WITHDRAWN
FROM STOCK

GREATEST
CHURCHES AND
CATHEDRALS
OF THE WORLD

IN ASSOCIATION WITH
TIMPSON

Also available

The 50 Greatest Prehistoric Sites of the World

The 50 Greatest Musical Places of the World

The 50 Greatest Bike Rides of the World

The 50 Greatest Dishes of the World

The 50 Greatest Wonders of the World

The 50 Greatest Road Trips

The 50 Greatest Westerns

The 50 Greatest Train Journeys of the World

The 50 Greatest Rugby Union Players of All Time

The 50 Greatest Beers of the World

The 50 Most Influential Britons of the Last 100 Years

The 50 Greatest Walks of the World

Geoff Hurst's Greats: England's 1966 Hero Selects His Finest Ever Footballers

David Gower's Greatest Half-Century

GREATEST
CHURCHES AND
CATHEDRALS
OF THE WORLD

SUE DOBSON

Published in the UK in 2017 by
Icon Books Ltd, Omnibus Business Centre,
39–41 North Road, London N7 9DP
email: info@iconbooks.com
www.iconbooks.com

Sold in the UK, Europe and Asia
by Faber & Faber Ltd, Bloomsbury House,
74–77 Great Russell Street,
London WC1B 3DA or their agents

Distributed in the UK, Europe and Asia
by Grantham Book Services, Trent Road,
Grantham NG31 7XQ

Distributed in Australia and New Zealand
by Allen & Unwin Pty Ltd,
PO Box 8500, 83 Alexander Street,
Crows Nest, NSW 2065

Distributed in South Africa by
Jonathan Ball, Office B4, The District,
41 Sir Lowry Road, Woodstock 7925

Distributed in India by Penguin Books India,
7th Floor, Infinity Tower – C, DLF Cyber City,
Gurgaon 122002, Haryana

Distributed in Canada by Publishers Group Canada,
76 Stafford Street, Unit 300, Toronto, Ontario M6J 2S1

Distributed in the USA by Publishers Group West,
1700 Fourth Street, Berkeley, CA 94710

ISBN: 978-178578-283-1

Images – see individual pictures

Typeset and designed by Simmons Pugh

Printed and bound in the UK by Clays Ltd, St Ives plc

ABOUT THE AUTHOR

Sue Dobson is an award-winning travel writer and magazine editor with a passion for discovering the world, its art, music, religions and cultures. A lifetime of travelling has taken her through all seven continents and her work is published in guidebooks, magazines and online. Home is a pretty village in the English countryside, but she's never happier than when out exploring – churches and cathedrals being high on her list of 'must-sees'. She is a member of the British Guild of Travel Writers and a Fellow of the Royal Geographical Society.

CONTENTS

INTRODUCTION

More than 10 million people visit England's cathedrals in a year and all over Europe church buildings regularly top visitor lists. No museum or art gallery, however large or impressive, can equal the sensation of looking up into the Bell Harry Tower at Canterbury Cathedral or stepping under the fan vaulting in King's College Chapel, Cambridge. Nothing can compare with experiencing the vast spaces of shimmering mosaics at Monreale, the acres of medieval glass at York or indeed imagining Giotto at work creating the glorious frescoes that cover whole walls in Assisi. The sheer beauty of so much art and artistry in one place can overwhelm the senses and the emotions.

Cathedrals inspire awe and wonder, not least for the incredible craftsmanship involved in their creation. Who were these people who centuries, even a thousand years ago, could not only visualise such grandeur but had the mathematical knowledge to make it happen and the skills to build it? Even today, with all the technology at our fingertips, architects and engineers still marvel at the construction of Ely Cathedral's octagon and lantern. Michelangelo and Brunelleschi looked to the 2nd-century Pantheon in Rome for knowledge and inspiration before constructing their own famous domes.

Visible from miles around, cathedrals dominate city skylines. Some, like London's St Paul's, St Vitus in Prague, Cologne's twin spires and the innovative Hallgrímskirkja in Reykjavík, are among a country's most iconic sights. Dotted across the countryside, church spires herald a distant town or village. If cathedrals tell the story of a city, a parish church is the repository of local history. Exploring them can be fascinating.

The great age of cathedral building began in the 11th century under the Normans. After the Conquest (1066) they quickly set about building or rebuilding England's great abbeys and cathedrals in the commanding Romanesque style that exuded power. Architecture favoured in northern France, it used rounded, semi-circular arches and massive columns and walls to support the weight of heavy roofs.

Then during the 12th century a new style emerged, again from northern France, with sophisticated techniques that would reduce the weight on walls via pointed arches, ribbed vaults and flying buttresses, allow for more window space and open up a raft of technical and engineering possibilities.

Now known as Gothic (actually a derogatory term invented much later), as architects and masons created ever more daring and complex designs, the Gothic pointed arch evolved through various incarnations into the 16th century and was revived in the early 19th. Buildings rose to ever more dizzying heights, decoration became ever more detailed and ornate.

It was during the high medieval period of the 12th and 13th centuries that most of Britain's and Europe's greatest cathedrals were constructed in the Gothic style that emphasised height and light. The building of them often spanned a century or more and it's interesting to see how new styles were incorporated as fashions in architecture changed.

After Gothic came Renaissance (and the invention of perspective in art, so clearly shown in Assisi and on the domes above the Choir of St Paul's) and the opulence of Baroque (the interior of St John's Co-Cathedral in Valetta, Malta being a prime example of over-the-top riches) before the return to more classical lines and modern architectural designs.

Ecclesiastical buildings suffered greatly after Henry VIII's break with Rome, during the English Civil War and as a result of the Reformation that spread across Europe. And yet most survived to rise again and tell their tales down succeeding centuries, continuing to delight and fascinate their millions of visitors.

Incidentally, what makes a Christian church a cathedral has nothing to do with size. Situated at the heart of a diocese, a cathedral is a bishop's church. It is the site of the bishop's chair ('cathedra', from the Latin for chair) or throne, symbol of the bishop's (or in some cases archbishop's) ecclesiastical and spiritual authority. Given that bishops were extremely powerful people in the Middle Ages, their churches had to be suitably grand in size and embellishment as befitted the importance both of the dignitary himself and of the Church in society.

Testimony to the skills of engineers and mathematicians, stonemasons and sculptors, carpenters and woodcarvers, fresco painters and stained glass artists, cathedrals and churches are treasure houses of art and history. Keeping these ancient buildings beautiful for our enjoyment and use as houses of prayer costs a fortune and many have resorted to charging entrance fees to visitors (though never to attend services or to drop in for quiet moments of prayer). How much poorer we would all be if they were allowed to crumble through lack of upkeep.

The choice of just 50 cathedrals and churches across the world is inevitably a personal one. Through these pages I hope you won't be too disappointed if your favourite is not included but rather find some interesting surprises.

Spanning the centuries, they have been chosen for their architectural and decorative interest as well as for the stories they have to tell so, while highlighting their history and standout features, I've tried to pinpoint the must-sees, the don't-miss elements of each one.

I hope you will enjoy reading about them but most of all, I hope this book will inspire you to go visiting and make your own wonderful discoveries.

THE 50 GREATEST
CHURCHES AND CATHEDRALS
OF THE WORLD

UNITED KINGDOM and IRELAND

– ENGLAND –

CHURCH OF CHRIST, CANTERBURY

The Mother Church of the worldwide Anglican Communion, and shrine to the rebirth of Christianity in England, is host to more than a million visitors a year. Every hour, on the hour, they are asked to be still and join in a prayer – a reminder that, spectacular though the building is, Canterbury Cathedral is very much a working church.

Huge and intricate, overpowering and dramatic, it is a multi-layered cathedral, each level reached by steps shaped by centuries of pilgrim feet. It was the brutal murder, at an altar in his own cathedral, of Archbishop Thomas Becket – by four of King Henry II's knights on 29 December 1170 – and accounts of miraculous healing immediately after his death, that brought the Christian world to its doors in the Middle Ages. Becket's was one of the holiest shrines in all Europe and pilgrimages continue to this day.

Founded in 597, it was rebuilt in 1070 and then largely rebuilt and extended in creamy-white Caen stone in 1178. A devastating fire four years earlier had demolished most of the previous cathedral, though the vast and atmospheric 11th-century crypt with its rounded arches and decorated columns, naves, aisles and side chapels, survives to present

Photo: Immanuel Giel

us with some of the finest Norman stone carvings on pier capitals in England.

They range from geometric to floral to entire stories that are often comical or violent. Look for animal musicians and winged beasts, rams' heads, knights doing battle and a rather appealing lion. The 12th-century wall paintings in the crypt's St Gabriel's Chapel, which include the Archangel Gabriel announcing the birth of John the Baptist to the elderly Zacharias, are the oldest known Christian paintings in the country.

Long, light, tall and graceful, the nave has slim, soaring columns rising to delicate vaulted arches and gilt roof bosses. Looking back you see the glorious west window, its stained glass dating back 800 years; ahead of you, a wide flight of steps leads up to the richly carved, 15th-century stone pulpitum (choir screen) that separates the nave from the choir. Within its niches are original effigies of six English kings that somehow escaped the swords of the Puritans who, during the Civil War of the 1640s, destroyed the accompanying statues of the twelve Apostles during their rampage of destruction through the cathedral. They even stabled their horses in the nave.

Through the screen's archway you get an inspirational view up to the high altar. Stand under the great Bell Harry Tower, and marvel at the stupendous fan vaulting high above you.

From the north-west transept, steps lead down to the Martyrdom Chapel. The site of Becket's murder is marked with a simple altar and a dramatic modern sculpture of jagged swords. Nearby, the circular Corona Chapel, built to house the skull fragment of the crown of the head of St Thomas Becket, sliced off by the sword of one of the attackers, is dedicated to saints and martyrs of our own times.

The powerful choir is Early French Gothic in style, built

between 1175 and 1185 and the first major example of Gothic architecture in Britain. The architect, master mason William (Guillaume) de Sens, was badly injured when he fell from scaffolding while inspecting the central roof boss – depicting a lamb and flag in blue and gold, a symbol of the Resurrection – in 1178. His assistant, William the Englishman, continued and completed the work, including the graceful Trinity Chapel behind the high altar.

The Trinity Chapel is where Becket's relics once rested in a magnificent gold and jewel-encrusted shrine, destroyed in 1538 on the orders of King Henry VIII. Cart loads of treasure boosted the royal coffers – a large ruby, given by the King of France, is now part of the crown jewels in the Tower of London.

Two years later, as part of the dissolution of the monasteries, Henry closed down the Benedictine monastery that had surrounded the cathedral since the 10th century. Today a solitary burning candle marks the site of the shrine; the flooring, with its beautiful Italian marble paving, survives and dates from 1220.

The chapel houses the tomb and superb bronze chain mailed effigy of Edward the Black Prince, eldest son of King Edward III and father of King Richard II, who died in 1376. His military victories, especially over the French in the Battles of Crécy and Poitiers, made him a popular figure at home (though not, unsurprisingly, in France, where he was considered an evil invader and occupier).

Opposite, lies his nephew, King Henry IV (d.1413), the only king to be buried in Canterbury Cathedral, and his wife, Joan of Navarre, Queen of England. Finely detailed alabaster effigies show them side by side, crowned in gold.

Trinity Chapel is also where you'll find St Augustine's Chair, the ceremonial enthronement chair of the Archbishop of Canterbury. Made from one piece of Petworth marble, it dates from the early 13th century.

Pilgrims to the shrine would have gazed in awe at the luminous stained glass of brilliant hue that portrays miracles attributed to the saint. Roundels in the aptly named Miracle Windows in the ambulatory begin with Becket at prayer and then a storyboard of scenes unfolds to tell of individuals who were cured of maladies from leprosy to blindness and myriad disabilities. Dating from the early 13th century, the colours are extraordinary – intense blue, striking reds, golden yellows, sharp greens – and the figures recognisably lifelike, studied yet full of movement.

Canterbury has a wealth of medieval stained glass. The colours are deep and vibrant and every image tells a story, whether biblical or of the cathedral's own history. Look especially for the Bible and the Miracle windows, but all of it will stop you in your tracks.

The west window is also known as the genealogy window for it contains images of early English kings and royal coats of arms, archbishops and, in the tracery lights, an array of apostles and prophets, all glass from the late 12th or early 13th centuries. The oldest (c.1174), Adam Delving in the Garden of Eden, showing Adam as a peasant tilling the soil, is in the bottom row.

In the north choir aisle, two 12th-century Bible windows tell Old and New Testament stories, from Noah releasing the dove to St Peter preaching, the Magi following the star to the parable of the sower and Christ's miracles, including the Marriage at Cana and the miraculous draught of fish.

When Pope Gregory sent St Augustine and his monks from Rome in 597, to restore the Christian faith to the Saxon English, they landed in Thanet and were welcomed by King Ethelbert (who would soon be baptised by Augustine) and his French Christian wife, Queen Bertha. Augustine was the first Archbishop of Canterbury.

A short walk from the cathedral lie the ruins of St Augustine's Abbey, founded in 598. The abbey, the cathedral and St Martin's church are a World Heritage Site and are linked by Queen Bertha's Walk. St Martin's, believed to date back to Roman times and the oldest church in continuous use in England, is where St Augustine came to worship before he established his monastery.

The cathedral's late medieval cloisters and large chapter house are remnants of the Benedictine monastic buildings. Originally set out by Archbishop Lanfranc in the 11th century and rebuilt in the early 15th, with their heavily ribbed lierne vaulted ceiling they are fine examples of the Perpendicular style – no surprise perhaps because they were remodelled by Stephen Lote, a pupil of the royal master mason Henry Yevele, who created the stunning nave. Roof bosses and heraldic shields tell of people who contributed to the rebuilding of the cathedral back in the 12th century and modern stained glass, installed in 2014, commemorates modern benefactors to the conservation of the building's fabric.

Lanfranc also built the rectangular chapter house with stone seating for the monks around the walls and a raised chair for the prior. Made from Irish oak, the beautiful early 15th-century wagon vaulted ceiling was given by Prior Chillenden, as were the stained glass windows that depict important people in the history of the cathedral.

The top row of the east window shows Queen Bertha, St Augustine and King Ethelbert. King Henry VIII appears second left on the bottom row. The west window depicts scenes from the history of the cathedral, including the murder of Archbishop Thomas Becket, the penance of

King Henry II and the move of Becket's bones to his shrine in 1220.

Entry to the cathedral and its precincts is via the impressive, turreted and highly decorated Christ Church Gate, one of the last parts of the monastic buildings to be erected before the Dissolution. Ironically, it may have been built to commemorate the marriage of Prince Arthur, elder brother of King Henry VIII, to Katharine of Aragon in 1502. (The young prince died a few months later and Henry went on to marry Katharine himself.)

Emerge from the gateway and take time to stand and stare. Of the cathedral's three pinnacled towers, the central Bell Harry tower rises supreme. It dates from between 1493 and 1503, is 72 metres (235 feet) high and is named after the original bell given by Prior Henry. Inside, the exquisite fan vault interior of the tower is one of the most glorious sights of this most memorable of cathedrals.

CATHEDRAL CHURCH OF THE BLESSED VIRGIN MARY, LINCOLN

Crowning the city, its three vast towers visible for miles, Lincoln's hilltop cathedral is one of the finest medieval buildings in Europe. It is huge – in terms of floor area, among English cathedrals only St Paul's in London (page 43) and York Minster (page 34) are bigger – and it presents a dramatic and elegant face to the world.

The 14th-century towers, delicate, lacy and topped with sky-piercing pinnacles, rise up behind the west front's 13th-century screen with its rows of Norman niches, Early

Gothic blind arcading and handsome Norman doors.

The towers today are an impressive height, but when the central tower collapsed in 1237 its replacement was topped with a spire, reputedly making Lincoln's cathedral the tallest man-made structure in the world, topping even Egypt's Great Pyramid at Giza. It held that record for 238 years, until the 160-metre (525-foot)-spire blew down in a raging storm in 1548 and wasn't replaced.

William the Conqueror ordered a cathedral to be built on the hill in Lincoln, sited next to his castle for security, and sent Bishop Remigius to supervise it. Constructed of locally quarried Lincolnshire limestone and consecrated in 1092, it commanded a vast diocese that stretched from the Humber estuary in the north to the River Thames in the south, spanning nine counties and encompassing several notable and wealthy monasteries.

After a devastating earthquake in 1185, Hugh of Avalon, a Carthusian monk of character, began the rebuilding of the cathedral, greatly enlarging it in the Early Gothic style, incorporating pointed arches, ribbed vaults, lancet windows and flying buttresses. Consecrated Bishop of Lincoln in 1186, he died in 1200 and was canonised in 1220 – in good time for the completion of the new cathedral, which saw pilgrims flocking to his shrine.

The long nave is soaring and lyrical, a space of beauty and light – especially when sunshine pours through the fine Victorian stained glass and dapples the limestone floor and piers with patterns of rich colour. Graceful arched stone ribs draw the eye heavenwards.

At the nave's end, the elaborate choir screen is a tour de force of early 14th-century carving, alive with beasts, heads and fantasy creatures among leaves and flowers.

The Bishop's Eye floods the great transept with light from

Photo: Tilman2007

on high. A magnificent circular rose window of precious medieval stained glass, its graceful tracery of leaves encases the glass with softly curving lines. Facing it on the north side, the earlier (13th-century) Dean's Eye rose window has four circles surrounded by sixteen smaller ones, with some of its original Last Judgement narrative still discernible.

Ornate 13th-century doorways lead to the choir aisles – look for dragons hiding behind foliage and the sword-bearing men seeking them out – and bring you towards a forest of exquisite wood and stone carving of heart-stopping delicacy.

The angels, carved on the choir desks around 1370, play harps, pipes and a drum; etched in gold above the canopied and pinnacled choir stalls with their secretive misericords are the first lines of psalms each canon was appointed to read.

The Treasury is located in the north side choir aisle. It was the first open Treasury in an English cathedral and as well as Lincoln's own silverware it contains other sacred pieces from churches around the diocese. The highlight is a medieval chalice hallmarked 1489.

Behind the high altar, the Gothic Angel Choir has a feast of stone carving and impressive stained glass windows. It was created to hold the shrine of St Hugh, whose following was so great that the cathedral had to be extended 80 years after his death to accommodate all the pilgrims. King Edward I and Queen Eleanor were among the great and the good that were there to see his body translated to the site prepared for him.

The infamous Lincoln imp has his place here among the host of presiding angels. The legend goes that the mischievous imp caused mayhem in the cathedral and when he started throwing rocks at the angels they turned him to stone. He may be quite difficult to spot high up in his spandrel, but his image has long been a symbol of the city.

The tomb of King Edward I's beloved wife Eleanor of Castile, who died near Lincoln in 1290, contains the viscera from her embalmed body, which was borne with great ceremony to London. The king decreed that a monument should be erected at each of the twelve towns where the funeral procession stopped overnight on its journey south. Being topped by tall crosses, they became known as 'Eleanor Crosses'.

Eleanor's Lincoln tomb, a replica of that in Westminster Abbey, was badly damaged in the English Civil War by Oliver Cromwell's forces during their siege of Lincoln in 1644 and the effigy seen above the stone chest is a 19th-century copy.

Among the many small chapels, some very poignant like the Airmen's Chapel that especially remembers the men of Bomber Command who flew from nearby airfields in the Second World War, the Russell Chantry stands out for its murals painted by Bloomsbury Group member Duncan Grant in the 1950s.

Although never a monastic foundation, the cathedral has a fan vaulted chapter house (1220) and relatively small but attractive cloisters (1295) with Gothic arches and a wooden ceiling. King Edward I conducted meetings of Parliament in the Chapter House on three occasions and the stained glass windows tell of events in the cathedral's history.

Above the cloisters, a thousand years of history are recorded in manuscripts and books. The 15th-century Medieval Library still retains many of its chained books and holds among its riches a 10th-century copy of homilies by the historian the Venerable Bede, hand painted atlases and a manuscript of Chaucer's *The Canterbury Tales*. The Wren Library, designed in 1674 by Sir Christopher Wren, the architect of St Paul's Cathedral (page 43), is a beautiful setting for a fascinating collection of early printed books, including 100 printed before 1501. The libraries are open to the public between April and October.

For centuries it was where one of the only four surviving copies of Magna Carta, signed by King John in 1215, was held. The then Bishop of Lincoln, Hugh of Wells, was one of those present for the sealing at Runnymede. It is now on permanent loan to nearby Lincoln Castle, but a facsimile copy can be seen near the cloisters.

The Victorian writer John Ruskin wrote: 'I have always held that the cathedral of Lincoln is out and out the most precious piece of architecture in the British Isles.' In its shadow, over Minster Yard, is the Medieval Bishop's Palace while across the square William the Conqueror's castle, dating from 1068, affords splendid views over the lower town and surrounding countryside.

CATHEDRAL CHURCH OF CHRIST, BLESSED MARY THE VIRGIN AND ST CUTHBERT, DURHAM

On its peninsula ridge above the wooded cliffs that rise up sheer from the fast-flowing River Wear, Durham Cathedral stands rock solid, a golden sandstone elegy to power and strength. Inside, that show of strength pervades in the unforgettable pillars that line the 11th-century nave. They are 6.6 metres (almost 22 feet) round, 6.6 metres high, and deeply carved in bold geometric patterns.

Full of architectural achievements way ahead of its time, the cathedral's early monastic history is revealed not least in the slab of black marble set in the nave's floor that marked the point beyond which no women were allowed to step.

Topped and tailed by two splendid chapels – the Galilee, or Lady Chapel at the west end with its 12th-century wall paintings, medieval glass and tomb of the great historian and scholar the Venerable Bede, and the spacious, stained-glass-filled Chapel of Nine Altars at the east end, overlooked by St Cuthbert's Shrine – it is a church of surprises.

There's vibrant, modern stained glass that reflects the local community's involvement in a church for today; its interest in the wider world is revealed by a beautiful banner from Lesotho in Southern Africa, woven to commemorate the cathedral's 900th birthday.

Prior Castell's glorious Tudor clock in the south transept dates from the early 16th century and survived the Civil War. It is huge, ornate, brilliantly colourful and tells the time of day, the day of the month and the phases of the moon. Look carefully at the face – it has 48 (instead of the usual 60) minute markings.

Much of the cathedral's colour comes from nature, from the swirls of cream, gold and orange in the sandstone walls and clear fossil patterns of the local Frosterley stone in pillars, to the boldly patterned marble floor of the choir.

The magnificent, intricate Neville Screen behind the high altar was carved from Caen stone in the 1370s. Behind that screen is the tomb of the gentle, holy St Cuthbert, the shepherd boy who became Bishop of Lindisfarne and brought the Christian faith to this area of North-east England. He died in 687 and is the reason the cathedral was built.

Cuthbert was revered in Lindisfarne (or Holy Island) but when it came under frequent attacks by Danes, the monks left to seek refuge in Northumbria, carrying with them the body of their Bishop. In 995, so the legend goes, the cart bearing the coffin suddenly stopped and could not be moved. Following a route taken by dairymaids searching for

a lost dun (brown) cow, they were led to a rocky outcrop above the river Wear, and once more the cart moved easily. Believing this to be a sign from Cuthbert that this should be his last resting place, the monks built a small church and shrine there. To this day, the road leading up to the hilltop site of Durham Cathedral is called Dun Cow Lane.

After the Norman Conquest in 1066, William I chose Durham as his preferred location from which to administer the north of his kingdom and protect it against invasion by raiding Scots. Seeing the defensive value of the position of the church holding the relics of the saint, which had by then become a popular pilgrimage site, he ordered the building of a castle, a monastery and a cathedral for the shrine of St Cuthbert.

Work began on the cathedral in 1093 under the command of William of St Calais, whom William the Conqueror had appointed to be the first Prince-Bishop. For the next almost 800 years, Durham's prince-bishops carried out a secular as well as a religious role, governing and protecting England's northern frontier, often more warriors than churchmen, living like kings and wielding significant power.

William's cathedral was constructed in a mere 40 years, although he did not live to see it, his work being completed by his ambitious successor, Bishop Ranulf Flambard. Although building continued into the 13th century, with the central tower rebuilt in the 15th, the interior of the cathedral we see today remains essentially Norman, a masterpiece of Romanesque architecture.

It's the nave with its avenue of powerful columns, dogtooth arches and decorative zigzagging that remains long in the memory of visitors, but look upwards and you will see one of the most daring innovations of the time.

English cathedrals of this period were built with wooden

roofs but Durham's vault is stone, with ribs forming pointed arches to support it, giving the effect of soaring lightness. It was an engineering achievement that marked a turning point in church architecture.

The cathedral suffered during the Reformation as zealots defaced statues and destroyed altars and stained glass. The riches of St Cuthbert's shrine were a prime target. In 1539 the commissioners who came to strip it of its treasure were amazed to discover that, just as the monks had always insisted, St Cuthbert's body was still intact in his tomb.

Today the shrine's simple grey stone, inscribed 'Cuthbertus', has an overhead canopy of vivid 20th-century colours and design. Depicting Christ as a young man, it is by the Scottish-born architect, Sir John Ninian Comper.

During the Civil War some 3,000 Scottish prisoners, captured by Oliver Cromwell, were held in the cathedral following the Battle of Dunbar in 1650. The conditions were appalling and all the woodwork in the great building was damaged or disappeared at this time. It's likely it was burned as firewood by the prisoners, at least half of whom died during their captivity. A mass grave was discovered during construction work on Palace Green, near the cathedral, in 2013.

After the Restoration of the English monarchy in 1660, it was Bishop John Cosin who replaced the choir stalls and towering cover of the marble baptismal font in a style that's a flamboyant mix of Gothic and Jacobean carving.

The Right to Sanctuary was abolished around this time. Under it, a person who had committed a great offence could rap the sanctuary knocker on the cathedral's northern door and be given refuge for 37 days, during which time they would try to reconcile with their enemies or arrange their exile on board a ship from the nearest port.

The original 12th-century sanctuary knocker with its lion-like face and bulging eyes is housed among the cathedral treasures; the one you see at the door now is a bronze replica.

The Benedictine monastery and its priory were closed down in 1539 during Henry VIII's Dissolution of the Monasteries, but the cathedral retains its cloisters (rebuilt in the 19th century) and boasts some of the most intact surviving 14th-century monastic buildings in England. These are now used to host Open Treasure, a £10 million visitor experience. The long, oak-beamed monks' dormitory is an exhibition space and library while the octagonal-shaped priory kitchen with its high rib-vaulted ceiling has been designed to provide a fitting home for the Treasures of St Cuthbert.

Across the green stands William the Conqueror's great motte-and-bailey castle, founded in 1072, the principal seat of Durham's Prince-Bishops for almost 800 years and now used by Durham University. Together with Britain's finest Norman cathedral, it is a UNESCO World Heritage Site.

YORK MINSTER

Vast, Gothic and boasting the biggest expanse of medieval glass in the world, the largest Chapter House and some of the finest windows in England, the Cathedral Church of St Peter in York (better known as York Minster), seat of England's second archbishop, isn't short on superlatives.

Its story goes back to a little wooden church hurriedly erected in 627 for the baptism of Edwin, King of Northumbria. He wished to wed the Christian princess Ethelburga of Kent and his conversion was a condition of the marriage. That church, rebuilt in stone and dedicated to St Peter, burned down; as did the next one. Invading Danes demolished the third church and it was only in 1080 that the north was sufficiently settled for the Norman Archbishop of York, Thomas of Bayeux, to begin work on rebuilding the Minster.

By the 13th century, however, its style of architecture was looking decidedly old fashioned and not considered impressive enough for the important city of York. The scale of the new Minster, finally dedicated in 1472, transformed it into the biggest medieval cathedral in England.

The exuberant west front has vast pinnacled towers; the great 15th-century tower rises in majestic simplicity. For all its size, the Minster's interior is surprisingly delicate and uncluttered, the awe-inspiring nave lit by immense windows. The nave's wooden vault, painted to look like stone, has bosses showing the life of Christ. They are Victorian replicas, replaced after one of the many fires that have dogged the building's history, but it's difficult to tell they are not originals.

York's stained glass is legendary. The west window, its heart-shaped centre created by glorious tracery and known as 'the Heart of Yorkshire' is stunning. Archbishops, saints and the principal events in the life of Christ range across its eight slender lancets, topped by the depiction of the Coronation of the Virgin and Christ in Majesty. It looks impressive from close up, but walk down the nave and look back to get the full impact.

Dominating the Lady Chapel, the east window, created nearly 70 years later in 1405, appears like a giant curtain of brilliance set in tiers of fine tracery. At over 23 metres (76 feet) high, it contains the largest single expanse of medieval stained glass in the world and amid angels, saints and

Photo: Gary Ullah

martyrs it combines stories from the Book of Genesis in the Old Testament and the Book of Revelation – the beginning and the end.

In the north transept, Early Gothic in style, the Five Sisters window dates from around 1260 and is the oldest complete window in the Minster. At 16 metres (53 feet), it is one of the tallest in England, and is composed of over 100,000 tiny panes dotted with colour. Look for the panel at the bottom depicting Daniel in the lion's den. It is Norman in origin and predates the window by a century at least.

The window was removed during the First World War to protect it from Zeppelin raids. When it was restored in the 1920s it was rededicated to the women of the British Empire who lost their lives in that war, the only such memorial in the country.

Nearby, an astronomical clock depicts the position of the sun and stars from the viewpoint of a pilot flying over York. Installed in 1955, it is dedicated to the aircrews who flew from nearby airfields during the Second World War and were killed in action.

High up in the south transept, the rose window is a remarkable survivor of the devastating fire of July 1984. The 7,000 pieces of glass were cracked in about 40,000 places, yet the window remained in one piece. The rescue work took three years to complete.

While the stonework that supports it is 13th century, the glass is a mix from the 16th, 18th and 20th centuries and includes red and white roses honouring the union of the Houses of Lancaster and York (Henry VII's marriage to Elizabeth of York in 1486) that ended the Wars of the Roses.

That the Minster's magnificent medieval glass survived the English Civil War was down to Yorkshireman Thomas Fairfax. When in 1644, York fell to Oliver Cromwell's forces after the decisive Battle of Marston Moor, the city was surrendered to the Parliamentarian commander on the condition that the cathedral wasn't damaged. Fairfax kept his promise. Today more than half of all the medieval glass in England is found here.

The 1984 fire destroyed the south transept roof with just six of the 68 vaulting bosses surviving the blaze. New ones were carved, including some designed by children to reflect 20th-century achievements and concerns. These include the moon landing, space exploration, a starving African child and saving the whale.

At the central crossing, gaze up to view the light and airy view of the tower vault and then take a look at the gilded detail on the pulpitum. Known as the King's Screen for its carved statues of kings of England from William the Conqueror to Henry VI, that there are fifteen of them means the doorway into the choir is off-centre. There's a theory that the screen was designed in 1420 to hold fourteen statues, but the early demise of Henry V in 1422, before the screen was finished, made the hasty inclusion of Henry VI necessary.

Linked by a vestibule from the north transept, the octagonal Chapter House is a masterpiece of construction. It has no central column – the ceiling is supported by timbers in the roof, an engineering technique that was revolutionary in the 13th century. Much of its 14th-century glass survives. Rising up to meet the vaulted roof, these beautiful big windows with their subtle geometric tracery flood the building with light. In the stone walls and canopies, strange beasts hide and myriad faces peep out from among beautifully carved foliage.

An impressive statue of the Christian-convert Constantine, who was acclaimed as Roman emperor by his troops in York (Eboracum) in 306, stands outside the Minster. The remains of the Roman barracks can be seen in the Undercroft as part of Revealing York Minster, a state-of-the-art museum that explores 2,000 years of history at the cathedral's site. Among the artefacts on public display for the first time is the 1,000-year-old illuminated manuscript known as the *York Gospels*.

CATHEDRAL CHURCH OF ST ANDREW, WELLS

Reached through ancient gateways, Wells Cathedral stands, gracefully triumphant, in its field of green. Its great west front – 45 metres (147 feet) wide, as broad as it is high, dating from around 1230 – is a sculpture gallery. Beneath a modern Christ in Majesty are rows of figures, many life-sized, representing bible stories and the resurrection theme, and layer upon layer of prophets and patriarchs, saints, apostles and angels. On a summer's evening, the creamy limestone setting for the largest gallery of medieval sculpture in the world turns warm and golden in the light of the setting sun.

Arguably the loveliest of the great English cathedrals, if the exterior is dramatic, the interior is a visual sensation. Your eye goes immediately to the pale, elegant strainer or 'scissor' arches at the nave crossing. Unique in English cathedrals, the simple yet stunning design looks modern, but in fact was an inspired 14th-century answer to the problem of a central bell tower unable to support the additional weight of a spire.

This is a much-used church, full of light and beauty. The pointed arches of the central nave are pleasingly proportioned while the simple vaulting reflecting the curve of the inverted (scissor) arches is delicately painted with an intricate Persian tree of life design.

Beautifully carved medieval capitals decorate columns in the aisles and transepts. Amid stylised foliage ('stiff-leaf') they picture moments in everyday life: a farmer chases a thieving fox, a cobbler hammers at a shoe, a man grimaces with toothache, boys steal grapes and get their come-uppance, a woman sews.

A passage and staircase in the south transept gives access to the library where the books date mainly from the 16th to the 18th centuries (earlier books and manuscripts were destroyed during the Reformation). Some are still chained to the book presses of 1686. Their subjects, ranging from theology to medicine, history, exploration and languages to science, reflect the interests of the clergy of that time.

In the north transept, look for the 24-hour astronomical clock which was installed around 1390. The outer circle of hours has twelve noon at the top, twelve midnight at the bottom; small gold stars mark the minutes in the second circle while the inner dial indicates the days of the month. A gold pointer shows the number of days since the New Moon. The clock's face displays the earth as the centre of the universe, the sun acts as the hour hand and on the quarter hour, jousting knights come out in tournament. Its medieval mechanism, replaced in 1837, is now in the Science Museum in London.

Windows bearing the cathedral's oldest stained glass, dating from around 1290, line a splendid staircase of well-worn steps that curves up to the octagonal Chapter House. Completed in 1306, it was where the business of the Dean and Canons (the Chapter) was conducted. Ribs of the high vaulted roof radiate from a central pillar, fanning out to meet those flowing from the half columns placed at each

Image: Neasy-Pic

corner of the octagon. Often compared to palm trees, the effect is of spacious elegance. Big windows are patterned with stone tracery but their original glass has mostly gone, smashed in the 17th century. Around the walls, nameplates indicate the Canons' seating arrangements, a decorative pointed arch defining each stall. Stone-carved faces smile out from between the canopies.

The soaring, ornate choir has been at the heart of the cathedral for over 800 years. Misericords hide beneath the wooden choir stalls. They date from the 1330s, each one carved from a single piece of oak, and depict animals, birds, humans and mythological figures set between two roundels of foliage. There's a cat chasing a mouse, a ewe feeding a lamb, a pair of parakeets in a pine tree and several figures appear to be doing what misericords do – supporting a seat.

Considered one of the most splendid examples of mid-14th-century stained glass, the great east window of the choir is often called the Golden Window for its glowing colours. It is a rare example of an intact Jesse Window of that period and shows Christ's family tree rising from Jesse, who was the father of King David. Being situated so high up probably saved it from destruction by the iconoclasts.

Wells was never a monastic foundation but does have cloisters, which were built over the first church that stood on this site back in 764. The stone-carved Saxon baptismal font survived and is in use in the cathedral.

Edging the peaceful lawns of Cathedral Green, picturesque Vicars' Close is a cul-de-sac of medieval houses and flower-filled gardens, built in 1348 to house the men of the choir. It is still home to members of the Vicars Choral.

Pass through the Penniless Porch and you are in the Market Place. William Penn, the founder of Pennsylvania, preached to a crowd of 3,000 souls here in 1685. Walking through the arched Bishop's Eye Gateway will lead you to the Bishop's Palace. In its splendid gardens are the wells that gave the town its name. Surrounded by high walls and a moat, entry is across a drawbridge complete with portcullis – and swans that summon food by pulling on a bell rope at the gatehouse.

Unlike most cities with a great cathedral, Wells is small. Sitting at the foot of Somerset's Mendip Hills, with peaceful views out over sweeping fields, trees and green countryside, it still retains many of its ancient buildings.

ST PAUL'S CATHEDRAL, LONDON

For all the towering modern architecture that's risen around it in recent years, St Paul's Cathedral remains dominant; Wren's great dome is instantly recognisable as a symbol of London. Watching over Ludgate Hill, 24 steps leading up to its main entrance on the majestic west front, the cathedral stands above the crowd at the highest point within the Square Mile that constitutes the City of London. The world of business and banking spreads out beyond the building's eastern limits.

Mellitus, Bishop of the East Saxons, erected a wooden building here in 604 and there's been a cathedral dedicated to the Apostle St Paul on this site ever since. Fires and Viking attacks demolished the early churches but a vast and splendid construction, begun around 1087 under the conquering Normans, survived, despite many vicissitudes, for almost 600 years. Plans were afoot to restore the dilapidated medieval cathedral when the Great Fire of

London in September 1666 changed everything. The catastrophic blaze, which destroyed two-thirds of the City of London including 13,200 houses and 87 parish churches, put it beyond repair.

Sir Christopher Wren – astronomer, scientist and mathematician, but much better remembered as a great architect – didn't have an easy time getting his plans for a new cathedral accepted. He produced his first design in 1669, but it took more designs and six years of wrangling before a decision was finally made. Royal approval, given by King Charles II for construction to begin in 1675, included the proviso that Wren could make adjustments when he deemed them necessary, a leeway he took to heart.

St Paul's was the first cathedral to be built in England after the Reformation and the first by a named architect. Wren lived to see the completion of his Baroque masterpiece; in his declining years he was hauled up in a basket to oversee work on the roof. After its completion in 1711, he often returned to sit under the dome in contemplation. He died in 1723 and is buried in the cathedral's crypt. Part of the inscription in Latin on his simple tomb reads: 'Reader, if you seek his monument, look around you'.

The view as you enter from the west front is of a sweeping vista down the long nave, encompassing the full extent of this vast cathedral. Behind you are the 9-metre (nearly 30-foot)-high Great West Doors, opened only on special occasions. The side aisles are lined with chapels and memorials, with the impressive monument to the Duke of Wellington, soldier, statesman and British military hero, placed in an arch between the nave and the north aisle.

St Paul's is built in the shape of a cross with, uniquely among English cathedrals, a dome crowning the intersection of its arms. Beneath it, the altar is encircled by seating for services. A highlight of a visit is to sit here and ponder the *trompe l'oeil* paintings high above, in which the figures, scenes and settings deceive the eye by appearing to be sculpted from stone. From 1715, the painter Sir James Thornhill spent the next four years working on these monochrome murals based on the life of St Paul.

The triangular spaces in the spandrels between the arches of the crossing are filled with mosaics depicting four Old Testament prophets and the evangelists Matthew, Mark, Luke and John. Designed by British artists, inspired by Roman art and created in a Venetian workshop, they were added in the mid- to late 19th century and are an introduction to the glorious mosaics to be seen in the choir and beyond.

Wren's iconic dome is a tour de force of engineering. At 111 metres (365 feet) high and weighing 65,000 tonnes, it is one of the largest cathedral domes in the world. Its innovative design consists of three distinct domes: the inner painted dome, the massive outer dome shell that dominated London's skyline and between the two, a brick cone that supports the ornate stone lantern above.

There are three gallery levels within this construction: around the inner painted dome, the quirkily acoustic whispering gallery is 252 steps up from the cathedral floor, while the stone gallery (376 steps up) and the golden gallery (528 steps up) encircle the outer dome and offer magnificent views across London for the fit and the brave with a head for heights.

In the 'arms' of the crossing, the highlight in the north transept is William Holman Hunt's painting *The Light of the World* (1900) and in the south transept, memorials to naval hero Horatio Nelson, artist JMW Turner and Antarctic explorer Captain Robert Falcon Scott.

Ahead there's the choir, its canopied choir stalls exquisitely

carved by Grinling Gibbons. The colourful mosaics covering the saucer domes of the ceiling depict the creation of the beasts of the earth, the fish of the sea and the birds of the air, seemingly supported by angels, arms aloft.

Covering the east end of the cathedral, the spectacular, vibrant mosaics were installed between 1894 and 1904 in response to Queen Victoria's complaint that St Paul's was 'dull, cold and dreary'. Shimmering in gold and glass, they were designed by the portrait artist William Blake Richmond, who had studied the art of mosaic in Italy, and tell Bible narratives from the Old and New Testaments.

High in the apse, the figure of Christ in Judgement, flanked by recording angels, watches over the modern (1958) high altar and ciborium (canopy) and the American Memorial Chapel, which commemorates those who gave their lives while on the way to, or stationed in, the UK during the Second World War.

Below ground, the crypt stretches the entire length of the cathedral and contains tombs and memorials to the great, the good and the famous of the land. The marble sarcophagus on Lord Nelson's tomb had been intended for Cardinal Wolsey, King Henry VIII's Lord Chancellor, but after his fall from favour when he failed to arrange the king's divorce from Katharine of Aragon, it remained unused until a suitable recipient could be found. The crypt's intricately patterned mosaic flooring was the work of inmates of women's prisons around London.

Considered 'the nation's church', St Paul's hosts events of national importance, from state funerals (Admiral Lord Nelson, the Duke of Wellington, Sir Winston Churchill, Margaret Thatcher) and services of thanksgiving after the end of wars and conflicts to happy royal occasions, including the wedding of Prince Charles to Lady Diana Spencer in

1981 and celebrations for Queen Elizabeth II's Silver, Gold and Diamond jubilees.

CATHEDRAL CHURCH OF THE HOLY AND UNDIVIDED TRINITY, ELY

Seen from a far distance across the flat Cambridgeshire fenland, Ely's cathedral seems almost ephemeral. Up close it is triumphant. The beautiful simplicity of the nave, the dizzying fan vaulting of the Octagon and Lantern Tower (one of the world's great architectural marvels), the sumptuous painted ceiling, glorious woodcarving and exquisite stone tracing make it a joy to visit.

Ely was an isolated island surrounded by marshland when St Etheldreda founded Ely Abbey in 672. A daughter of King Anna of East Anglia and one of England's earliest female saints, despite two arranged marriages she kept her vow of perpetual virginity and founded a dual monastery for monks and nuns at Ely, ruling as the Abbess. She died in 679 and when her coffin was opened years later, her body was found to be uncorrupted and even the cloths she was wrapped in appeared fresh. Her tomb became a popular medieval pilgrimage site, miracles were ascribed to her and the dates of her birth and death are celebrated in the cathedral to this day.

Etheldreda's abbey was sacked by the Danes then refounded as a Benedictine monastery for men in 970. It became one of the richest monasteries in England but was demolished in 1081 by the elderly Abbot Simeon, a relative of William the Conqueror, in order to build an impressive church in the Norman style. It would be a brilliant beacon of faith amid the lawless fens. Before it was even completed it had been designated a cathedral, with the first Bishop of Ely appointed in 1109.

Built from stone brought from Peterborough Abbey's own quarry at Barnack, and Purbeck marble from Dorset for decorative detail, it is renowned as an outstanding example of English Gothic architecture. A tall (66 metres, 215 feet) castellated and imposing tower with top-to-toe blind arcading dominates the west front; the two turrets of the south-west transept would not look amiss on a fairy tale castle.

Entrance to the cathedral is though the elegant great west door in the Galilee porch. A pavement labyrinth lies boldly beneath the tower. Added in the 19th century, the only one to be found in an English cathedral, it is 6.1 metres (20 feet) across and, unlike a maze, there are no confusing dead ends. To your left, look for 'The Way of Life', a contemporary sculpture in cast aluminium commissioned for the millennium. To your right, the south-west transept is a feast of Romanesque decoration.

Ahead is the long (75 metre, 248 foot) and stunning nave. With twelve bays, alternating in design, and three arcades of rounded arches supported by powerful piers, its cluster pillars rise right up to the clerestory and thus emphasise its height (32 metres, 105 feet). It dates from the early 12th century. The colourful, elaborately painted ceiling, however, is from the major restoration that took place in the mid-19th century. Based on the ancestry of Jesus, it begins with the creation of Adam and ends with the ascended Christ in Majesty, with Old and New Testament narratives, prophets and evangelists to seek out along the way.

There's a wonderful space at the top of the nave and its style is unique to Ely. In 1322, the Norman central tower collapsed, taking with it the crossing and three bays of the choir. It was a disaster that led to the cathedral's most famous and celebrated feature, the Octagon.

Through the imagination of the monk/architect Alan of Walsingham, working with the royal master carpenter William Hurley, the replacement of the old square tower with a stone octagon crowned by a lantern in wood, lead and glass to suffuse it with light, was not only revolutionary, it was a masterpiece of medieval engineering. It took eighteen years to build and the method of its construction still enthrals architects and engineers. To take a tower tour and get the view down onto the cathedral below is a memorable experience.

On either side of the Octagon, the north and south transepts are the oldest part of the building and contain fine stonework. Look up – the hammer-beam roofs, installed in the 15th century, are decorated with colourful flying angels.

The south transept chapel is dedicated to the two 10th-century bishops who founded the men's monastery in 970, St Dunstan and St Ethelwold. The Benedictine community remained until 1539 when it was disbanded during King Henry VIII's dissolution of the monasteries.

The rebuilding required by the tower's collapse offered the opportunity to rethink the first three bays of the choir, resulting in a style closer to that of the new Octagon. The rest of the choir stalls are 14th century and have carved wood misericords beneath the seats. These display whole tableaux, from Adam and Eve to the beheading of John the Baptist, as well as single figures of saints and musicians, animals and birds. The desks and front stalls have some fine Victorian-era carvings.

King Henry III and Prince Edward were in attendance when the presbytery behind the choir was dedicated in 1252.

Photo: Michael D Beckwith

The Victorian architect, George Gilbert Scott, designed the Italianate reredos of the high altar during his major restoration of the cathedral, which by the 19th century had fallen badly into disrepair. The delicate choir screen is his, too, and became a model for his work in churches and cathedrals around the country.

The far eastern end of the cathedral is dedicated to St Etheldreda. Elaborate, highly ornate chantry chapels grace the choir aisles, and a millennium project Processional Way in the north choir aisle restored the pilgrims' direct link to the Lady Chapel.

Added in the early 14th century and the largest attached to any British cathedral, the Lady Chapel was originally sumptuously decorated with statues, murals and stained glass windows. Today it is a sad reminder of the desecration wrought during the Reformation in the 16th century, but its vast size, light and airiness still have great impact. Arched alcoves line the walls, with exquisite filigree carvings, elaborate tracery and sinuous lierne vaulting on high. The modern statue of Mary above the altar has few admirers.

Most of the stained glass in Ely Cathedral dates from the mid-19th century restoration, when over 100 new windows were installed. To see older glass you should visit the cathedral's excellent Stained Glass Museum in the south Triforium. The only museum in Britain dedicated to stained glass, its collection of over 1,000 panels and windows spans the 13th century to the present day.

CATHEDRAL CHURCH OF ST PETER, ST PAUL AND ST ANDREW, PETERBOROUGH

Peterborough Cathedral's west front – a vast, Gothic, triple-arched portico as wide as it is tall – is unique in Christendom and the 13th-century painted nave ceiling unique in size and age in all Europe. Katharine of Aragon is buried here; Mary, Queen of Scots was interred here after her beheading at nearby Fotheringhay Castle. At the heart of the busy, ever-expanding city, the cathedral and its precincts are an island of serenity in a sea of shops.

When the first church was founded here in 655 in the reign of the Anglo-Saxon King Paeda, it was a monastic settlement on the edge of the remote and waterlogged fens. A largely uninhabited area, it was well stocked with fish, wildfowl and reeds for thatching. There was a fine quarry a few miles away at Barnack and timber could be had from Rockingham Forest, with the River Nene handy for transport.

Viking raiders destroyed the settlement in 870, the monks were killed and Christianity all but wiped out in the region as the Danish settlers had their own gods. Around a century later, Ethelwold, Bishop of Winchester, founded an abbey and monastery on the site under the Rule of St Benedict. Dedicated to St Peter, it thrived until an accidental fire swept through it in 1116.

Work began in 1118 on the Abbey Church that would become Peterborough Cathedral and, additions and renovations aside, the structure of the building has remained essentially as it was when it was consecrated in 1238.

Given the dramatic west front, the visitor could be forgiven for thinking that the rest might be a bit of a let-down. But

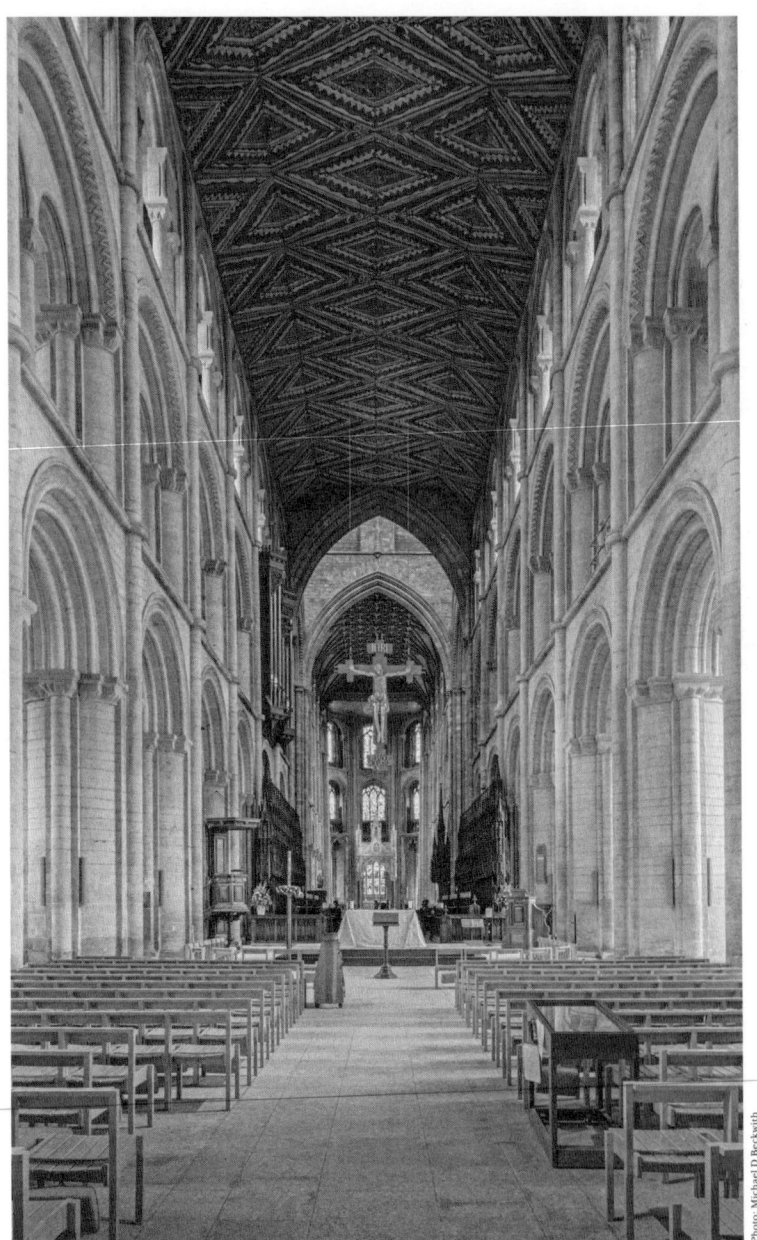

no, it more than lives up to its promise, for this is one of the finest Romanesque church interiors in the world.

Blessedly clear of clutter, the vista down the long, light and airy nave is of an arcade of wide curving arches and sturdy shafted piers, cool and solidly grounded in creamy Barnack stone. They rise in three storeys to the glorious wooden ceiling, hand painted between 1230 and 1250 and composed of lozenge panels, each one containing a different image. In darkly medieval colours, although the ceiling has been painted over twice, the design and pattern are original. Wheel one of the mirrored trolleys along to see the detail more clearly.

Made and erected in the 1970s, a huge wooden cross with the powerful figure of Christ in gold on a bright red background, is a striking focal point above the central altar at the end of the nave. In contrast, the bowl of the font at the cathedral's entrance, carved from local Alwalton marble, is from the 13th century. It was rescued from a nearby garden in the 1820s where it had been used as a flower tub. Look for the fish tucked in among the lilies and leaves.

High up on the wall behind you, Old Scarlett, a celebrated local character, is commemorated in a portrait, rhyme and faded fresco. The local gravedigger, he died in 1594 at the age of 98, his claim to fame being that he buried two queens in the cathedral. Legend suggests that he was the inspiration for the gravedigger in Shakespeare's *Hamlet*. Watching over all who enter and leave the building, he is portrayed in 'strength and sturdye limm', his spade in one hand, his keys in the other, and a skull at his feet.

A fine golden eagle lectern from the late 15th century stands boldly at the entrance to the choir with its beautifully hand-carved oak choir stalls full of exquisite lace-like detail. The lectern survived the ravages of the English Civil

War when the cathedral and the town (with its Royalist sympathies) suffered badly under Cromwell's brutish troops in 1643.

The story goes that the iconoclasts, told that the weighty lectern wasn't made of gold, snipped off a bit of its feathered wing to make sure. Satisfied that it wasn't such rich pickings after all, and being heavy to cart off, they left it behind, exhausted perhaps by the two days it had taken to demolish the elaborate stone pulpitum (screen) and its organ. By the time the Parliamentarians had finished their work, nearly all the cathedral's stained glass had been destroyed, the library's fine collection of books and manuscripts burned and the cloisters and Lady Chapel demolished.

The crossing is pure Norman, its north and south transepts unaltered except in their window glass – don't miss the brightly coloured 19th-century windows by Dante Gabriel Rosetti in the south transept.

In this transept are three small chapels, the most decorated being that dedicated to St Oswald, which even has a watching tower from which monks could safeguard what had been Peterborough's most cherished relic – the arm of St Oswald (stolen, 'tis said, in the year 1000 from Bamburgh Castle by an abbey monk in an attempt to gain favour with his abbot). It disappeared during the Reformation.

The central tower has been rebuilt twice, most recently in the 19th century when pieces of falling masonry made the cathedral unsafe. The beams and the roof bosses of the very fine 14th-century wooden ceiling were replaced and it's a neck-cracking but joyous view from below.

The great Romanesque arcade of arches continues into the sanctuary where the high altar has an impressive – if somewhat incongruous – intricately carved, pink marble ciborium (altar canopy). It was added in the 1880s when the whole central and eastern end of the building required refurbishment after the rebuilding of the central tower.

The sanctuary has a fine marble tesserae pavement and overhead a stunning early 16th-century vaulted ceiling panelled in navy blue and gold. The sky blue and gold ceiling painting of Christ in Majesty was restored at the same time, having suffered from Parliamentarian musket shot.

Alongside the sanctuary, two Tudor queens are remembered. In the north aisle, Katharine of Aragon, discarded first wife of King Henry VIII, is given the dignity of her title Queen of England above the simple marble slab that indicates her grave. Peterborough was the nearest abbey to Kimbolton Castle, where she died in January 1536, and every year a service is held here in her memory.

The body of another sad queen, Mary, Queen of Scots, was brought to Peterborough five months after her execution at Fotheringhay Castle in 1587. In 1612 her remains were exhumed and taken to Westminster Abbey for reburial on the orders of her son, King James I of England. Her memorial is in the south aisle.

Ahead, the magnificent 'New Building' is a whirl of fabulous fan vaulting by the leading Tudor architect John Wastell, a design he went on to develop further for the ceiling of King's College, Cambridge (page 62). Built in the early 1500s as a processional route around the east end of the building, it contains some interesting stained glass windows and the Hedda Stone. A grave marker for Abbot Hedda and his monks, murdered by the Danes when they sacked the original abbey, the Hedda Stone is believed to date from 870.

Peterborough Abbey was dissolved in 1539 during the Reformation and its land and properties confiscated. Instead of tearing down the church, however, King Henry VIII created a new bishop (the former abbot) in 1541 and the great abbey was transformed into Peterborough Cathedral.

ST MICHAEL'S CATHEDRAL, COVENTRY

The German Luftwaffe's prolonged bombing raid on Coventry on the night of 14 November 1940 devastated the historic city. As the incendiary bombs rained down, its cathedral burned with it. The next morning, Richard Howard, the visionary Provost of the time, put his hand in the ashes and wrote the words 'Father forgive' on the blackened wall of the sanctuary. He vowed to rebuild the cathedral as a sign of faith, trust and hope for the future of the world and to work for reconciliation.

Before it was designated Coventry's cathedral in 1918, St Michael's, dating from the 14th century, had been the largest parish church in England, a wonder of Perpendicular Gothic architecture. Its windows were painted by John Thornton who went on to work on the glass in York Minster (page 34).

While most of the building lay in ruins, the splendidly carved 15th-century tower and spire stood their ground and together with the shell of outer walls and skeletal tracery form a dramatic, thought-provoking ensemble framed against the sky. The 90-metre (295-foot)-spire is still the tallest structure in the city.

In 1950, over 200 architects submitted drawings in the competition held to design a new cathedral. Basil Spence, later knighted for his work, won with his plan to keep the ruins as a garden of remembrance and to incorporate them into the design of the new building.

His use of the same pink-red Staffordshire sandstone expressed continuity and brought visual unity to the ensemble. Spence's determination to have the new building seemingly arising from the ruins of the old meant that the cathedral must face north/south (instead of the traditional east/west alignment).

Queen Elizabeth II laid the foundation stone in March 1956 and the new cathedral was consecrated in her presence in May 1962. To mark the occasion, Benjamin Britten's specially composed *War Requiem* received its premiere in the cathedral.

At the entrance, a monumental porch and steps link the old and new structures. A 21-metre (70-foot)-high clear glass screen, engraved with Old and New Testament figures, saints, martyrs and angels, allows visitors to view the inside of the new cathedral with a reflection of the old.

Guarding the steps, a powerful bronze sculpture, St Michael and the Devil, symbolises the strength of good over evil. Depicting the archangel standing triumphant and victorious over a cowering Lucifer, it is by Sir Jacob Epstein, one of several leading British artists and sculptors of the time to contribute fine work to the new cathedral.

Stained glass windows angled in zigzag walls direct light down the nave towards the altar and the immense tapestry, Christ in Glory. Designed by Graham Sutherland, who in the preceding years had worked as an official war artist recording the effects of German bombing on Britain, it measures 23 metres x 11.5 metres (75 feet x 38 feet), and weighs over a tonne. Woven near Aubusson in France and using about 900 colours, it is said to be the largest tapestry in the world to be woven in one piece.

Drawing on the Byzantine Christ Pantocrator, the image is of a very human Christ, risen in glory, hands raised in blessing, eyes encompassing all before him. He is flanked by the traditional symbols of the four evangelists; the human figure at his feet seems tiny, but in fact is life-sized.

Of brilliant hue and full of symbolism, the ten 21 metre-(70 foot)-high angled side windows only become visible when you walk back down the nave from the altar but John Piper's phenomenal Baptistry window (to your right as you enter the cathedral) has immediate impact.

An entire wall of stained glass, its vivid colours moving from the outer reds, blues and greens to a sunburst of gold and white at the centre, each of the 195 individual windows contains an abstract design and the overall effect is mesmerising. A large boulder brought from a hillside near Bethlehem forms the font at its feet.

Following the aisle from the Baptistry to the altar brings you to the serenely beautiful Chapel of Christ in Gethsemane. Seen through a crown of thorns made from iron, it shows a kneeling angel in gold mosaic offering the cup of suffering to Christ as he prays.

Provost Richard Howard's vision back in 1940 was for a new cathedral that would be at the heart of a movement for peace and reconciliation between all people of all faiths. Seeing how in wartime Christians of all denominations came together to pray, he conceived the idea of an ecumenical space within the new cathedral – a revolutionary idea at the time. It came to fruition in the Chapel of Unity, a star-shaped building attached to the cathedral. Its colourful mosaic floor, donated by the people of Sweden, represents the nations of the world and is lit by shafts of light from narrow, stained glass windows.

Coventry Cathedral has indeed become a global symbol of peace and reconciliation, not least in its Community of the Cross of Nails that furthers the work of global peace and

Photo: Steve Cadman

dialogue. After the destruction of 1940, Howard fashioned a cross from three nails he found in the medieval roof timbers and since then similar crosses have been given to churches around the world, symbolising new life and friendship out of enmity. One is in the wonderful Kaiser Wilhelm Memorial Church in Berlin, destroyed by Allied bombing, and like Coventry rebuilt as a contemporary church integrating the ruins of the old.

It was a controversial building from the start, and still divides opinion, but a national poll in 1990 showed Coventry Cathedral to be the UK's favourite 20th-century building and it is listed as one of 21 British landmarks for the 21st century.

KING'S COLLEGE CHAPEL, CAMBRIDGE

Painted by Turner and Canaletto, praised in verse by William Wordsworth, King's College Chapel is a gem in a city of standout architecture. Begun in 1446, it took nearly 100 years to build, involving five successive kings, four master masons and countless skilled craftsmen.

Entering through the north porch you are immediately immersed in the spacious vastness of the Chapel. The long, exquisitely beautiful fan vaulting – that intricate lacework of stone that was a uniquely English contribution to Gothic architecture – seems to float above the spectacular stained glass windows. Measuring 88.5 metres (289 feet) in length, it is 12.6 metres (40 feet) wide and was completed in a mere three years, from 1512 to 1515.

The finely sculpted side walls are decorated with heraldic carvings and Tudor symbols, the boldest being the Tudor rose. Incorporating the red rose of the triumphant House of Lancaster and the white rose of the House of York, it's the symbol of the union of Henry VII and Elizabeth of York, the marriage that brought together the two factions in the civil wars that became known as the Wars of the Roses.

Look too for the lattice grille portcullis and greyhound, emblems of the Beaufort family, Lady Margaret Beaufort being King Henry VII's mother; the Welsh dragon of Henry VII's father's family and the fleur de lys, a reminder that English kings had also been kings of France. The Royal Arms of King Henry VII appear frequently. Worshippers would have been left in no doubt of the power and importance of the Tudors.

Side chapels tuck in alongside, their entrance stone steps worn by the tread of centuries, their windows containing fragments of medieval glass. Don't miss the 16th-century triptych of scenes from Christ's early life in the Founder's Chapel.

Ahead, the triumphal, heavily carved and decorated choir screen in dark English oak was the gift of King Henry VIII. A superb example of Tudor woodwork, it is filled with stylised flowers, masks, strange creatures and heraldic badges, all studded with the king's initials (HR, Henricus Rex) and those of his second queen, Anne Boleyn (AR, Anna Regina). In places their initials are intertwined, bound up in a lovers' knot. As they were married in 1533 and Anne was executed three years later, this boldly romantic declaration gives a clear indication of the period during which the screen must have been designed and installed. Above it, angels trumpet from atop the gilded pipes of the great organ.

A splendid double-sided and beautifully engraved brass lectern greets you as you enter the choir. The gift of Robert Hacumblen, Provost of King's College in the early 16th

century and much involved with the building of the Chapel, it is topped with a statuette of the chapel's founder, King Henry VI, bearing an orb and sceptre.

The long rows of choir stalls were probably installed around the same time as the screen but their canopies and the heraldic carved panels behind them date from the 17th century. The magnificent painting of *The Adoration of the Magi* by Sir Peter Paul Rubens is the focal point of the high altar. The choir was the first part of the chapel to be built and, lacking the Tudor bombast of the antechapel, reflects King Henry VI's plan for simplicity.

When King Henry VI established King's College in 1441, his stated wish was for a choir to provide the music for the offices and celebrations in his new chapel. Today King's College Choir is famed worldwide, known especially for 'A Festival of Nine Lessons and Carols', broadcast live on Christmas Eve, and for their international tours and recordings. During term time the choir, comprising sixteen boy choristers aged between nine and thirteen years, and fourteen male undergraduates, sing daily Chapel services. To hear Evensong sung here is a memorable experience, well worth queuing up for.

King's College Chapel is blessed with 26 vast windows, twelve on each side flanked by an east and a west window. Lit by sunshine, their jewel-like colours bathe the interior with warmth. The work of Flemish glaziers, each window demands time to simply stand and stare. The glass is original, a rare survival of the Reformation, making it the finest collection of 16th-century stained glass in England.

Packed with detailed figures the windows depict scenes from the Old and New Testaments, many emphasising events that link the two by prefiguring or symbolising the coming and life of Christ. The east window gives the narrative of the

Passion and Crucifixion. They were all completed between 1515 and 1547, except the great west window, which shows the Last Judgement and dates from the mid-19th century.

The Chapel is one of the finest and most complete late Perpendicular Gothic buildings in Britain, constructed in three separate phases between 1446 and 1515, a tumultuous period in England's history that spanned the Wars of the Roses (1455–87). Installing the stained glass windows took a further 30 years.

King Henry VI, known for his piety and religious devotion, drew up a design for the chapel in 1448 and detailed how it was to be built, decorated and funded. It was to be 'without equal in size and beauty', a simple, grand statement, unencumbered by superfluous decorative details. The simple rectangular ground plan is very much as he stipulated, but it's unlikely that he would have approved of some of the decoration that was to come.

After his murder in the Tower of London in 1471, building work continued sporadically under King Edward IV and more intensely under King Richard III. By the time of Richard's death at the Battle of Bosworth in 1485, the first five bays of the Chapel were already in use.

Two Tudor kings completed and made their mark on this glorious work of art and craftsmanship. Building work began again in earnest in 1508 under King Henry VII, who sent some of the money to pay for it in the strong wooden chest bound with iron that's now on display in the Chapel Exhibition. He left generous funds in his will to cover the cost of the stonework, including master mason John Wastell's great fan vault, and some of the glazing. Finally his son, King Henry VIII, made his contribution with the magnificent carved oak choir screen, the choir stalls and the great glass windows.

An excellent exhibition in the north side chapels charts the construction stages and methods, shows how the glass was made, makes sense of the period and puts everything into context.

ST MARY THE VIRGIN, WELLINGBOROUGH

Tucked alongside a terrace of red-brick houses at the east end of an unremarkable East Midlands town, St Mary's appears to be an ordinary parish church, large but perhaps only of passing interest.

Appearances can be deceptive, however, for it was designed by Sir John Ninian Comper, one of the most influential and arguably the greatest among British church architects of the 20th century. The interior is sensational.

Comper considered St Mary's to be his finest work, certainly his favourite, and expressed his wish to be buried there with his wife. In the event, after his death in 1960 at the age of 96, such was his fame that his ashes were interred at Westminster Abbey – suitably placed beneath the windows he'd designed in the north aisle of the nave.

Entering under a severely plain, neatly crenellated tower of golden ironstone, nothing prepares you for the huge space, flooded with light, the amazing fan vaulting, the glorious gilded rood screen and the enveloping sense of calm to be found within. The plan is simple: Perpendicular Gothic with a broad nave, transept, chancel and two full-length side aisles with chapels attached. It's the design detail, the use of colour and the impact the church has on the visitor that makes it so special.

A committed Gothic Revivalist, Comper's journeys in Europe in the early 1900s led him to the conclusion that the beauty he sought to embody in Christian architecture need not be reliant on the medieval tradition but could incorporate the best of other architectural styles, too, and thus be universal. He called this drawing together 'unity by inclusion'. His other abiding belief was that a church should be functional. His was liturgy-driven architecture.

'The purpose of a church,' he wrote in 1917, 'is to move to worship, to bring a man to his knees, to refresh his soul in a weary land.'

Built between 1906 and 1931, and eventually consecrated in 1968, St Mary's is a fine example of these ideals. Eight bays of tall, octagonal columns of warm local stone lead the eye through the ornate screen and gilded rood loft to the altar, reverently canopied by a gold-pillared ciborium, and finally the stained glass windows shimmering in the distance. The simplicity of the nave's furnishings allows the most sacred parts of the church to leap instantly into focus.

Overhead, the highly decorated fan vaulting, its plaster dripping with pendants and studded with delicate bosses interlinked with snowflake-like roundels, feels surprisingly light in its whiteness. Stretching the entire length of the centre of the church, its detail is highlighted in gold and blue above both ends of the nave (baptismal font, high altar) and the screen – pinpointing their importance and offering an intimation of the vibrant colour that Comper originally planned for the whole church.

The classical worlds of Greece and Rome, the Italian Renaissance, English Gothic and medieval Byzantium all find their influences here.

The gloriously gilded rood screen with its gold and blue painted Tuscan columns and exquisitely decorated spandrels

Photo: Sue Dobson

is surmounted by a filigree-fronted Gothic loft and crucifix, golden angels with scissor-folded wings and a fresh-faced Christ in Glory, the Pantocrator, ruler of all, presiding from on high.

Wrought iron screens, inspired by the *rejas* of Spanish cathedrals such as Seville (page 213), surround the sanctuary and are full of delightful Gothic Revival detail. The entwined initials of the three sisters, Gertrude, Harriet and Henrietta Sharman, the unmarried daughters of a local landowner, who in 1904 commissioned Ninian Comper to design a 'modest' church to serve the needs of the rapidly expanding town, appear on the screens closest to the high altar.

Painted with decorative garlands of blue flowers, the gilded Corinthian columns supporting the ciborium above the altar are topped with praying angels, with a sunburst of the Risen Christ at the canopy's centre. Impressive though this structure is, it hides some rather lovely stained glass in the window behind it. Comper used family and friends as models for his figures. The serene Virgin Mother and Child statue nearby have the features of his wife and son.

To the left of the sanctuary, the Holy Name of Jesus Chapel was the first part of the church to be completed and was dedicated in 1908. Here you get the full impact of Comper's flamboyant use of colour. The ceiling is panelled, painted in blue, dotted with Tudor roses and decorated with golden angels in full flight. The stained glass window is a Tree of Jesse showing Christ's genealogy and the image of Mary, His mother, is modelled on a photograph of Grace Comper, Ninian's wife, whose ashes are buried here along with those of the architect's nephew and assistant, Arthur Bucknall, and his wife Ruth.

Over in the much simpler south chapel, dedicated to St John the Evangelist, some striking stained glass windows depict men and women who suffered for their faith in different eras, from Katharine of Aragon to a set of Tractarian priests. Both chapels are in use for daily services, one for summer, one for winter.

Showing a Greek influence, the stone pillars rise in shades of the earth; the pleasing entwined vines and lily design of their capitals can be fully appreciated in the few that are painted. Comper's plan was for much more of the interior to be painted and gilded, but the money ran out, so we are tempted by what could have been by illustrative sections in colour, like the panelled aisle roofs patterned with black, red and white chevrons.

At the west end of the nave, the distinctive font and baptistry are magnificent, surrounded by an octagonal screen of carved and gilded dolphins and adorned with an elegant canopy. Sebastian, Ninian Comper's architect son, completed them as a memorial to his father.

This is an unexpected find in an unlikely setting. A vicar friend calls St Mary the Virgin in Wellingborough the finest parish church in England. He could be right.

ST KYNEBURGHA, CASTOR

Sometimes you find a church that appeals, stays long in the memory and becomes a favourite. The Church of St Kyneburgha in the leafy Cambridgeshire village of Castor is mine.

It's the only church known to be dedicated to the saint, a Saxon princess, erstwhile queen of Northumbria and daughter of Penda, the pagan King of Mercia. Her brothers

Photo: Richard Humphrey

built the original abbey at Peterborough (page 53) and in 650 Kyneburgha, together with her sister Kyneswitha, founded a convent in the Celtic tradition, with monks and nuns, on the ruins of a Roman palace. The Vikings sacked it in the 10th century.

Castor was a suburb of the sprawling Roman city of Durobrivae, spreading over the south bank of the River Nene and famed for its distinctive 'Castor Ware' pottery, which was exported throughout the empire. When the palace was built in 250 AD, replacing a 1st-century villa, it was the second largest Roman building in Britain.

The Norman church was built over its courtyard; part of its temple lies under the Garden of Remembrance. Fragments of this long history, unearthed by those tending the gardens, are displayed in the church, alongside the stump of a pagan temple column re-used by the Saxons as the base for a cross.

Rare breed sheep are the official grass-mowers here, quite unfazed by the sloping terrain. Chosen because these breeds were known in the 12th century, which is when this lovely church was built, they're an appealing sight grazing between headstones and snoozing in the sun.

On a low hill, set back from the road and curtained by trees, St Kyneburgha's could be a textbook of medieval architecture. Dating from 1120 and built on Saxon foundations, it boasts arguably the finest Norman parish church tower in England, its two tiers of arcading impressively decorated and full of detailed carving. Many a cathedral would be envious of that workmanship.

Above the south porch a late-Saxon, stone-carved Christ in Majesty, flanked by the sun and moon, hands raised in blessing, beckons visitors into the Norman-arched entrance with its ancient and very heavy oak door. Inside all is light and cheering colour, graced by an angel roof; carved into the oak roof beams of the central nave, twelve brightly painted angels with outstretched gilded wings are clothed in colourful gowns. They carry musical instruments – pan pipes and violins, flutes, tambourines and mandolins – and represent the 'whole company of heaven'. The side aisles, too, have angel figures, regally bearing shields, books and musical instruments. Altogether there are over 60 of these angelic figures and they date from around 1450.

The sweeping Romanesque arches and sturdy clustered piers that line the nave have intriguing early-12th-century carved capitals. On the tower piers look for fighting men, birds, beasts and stylised foliage, St Kyneburgha seeing off men with evil intentions and several variations of the Green Man.

At the back of the north aisle, a 14th-century wall painting depicts scenes from the life of St Catherine. In the top panel she is seen converting some of the emperor's philosophers, the second panel shows them being executed and the third panel has St Catherine with the wheel that broke at her touch, when it was meant to kill her.

An 8th-century stone carving of St Mark that was probably on St Kyneburgha's original shrine stands by the altar dedicated to her sister, St Kyneswitha.

Beautifully stitched kneelers add much colour and interest to the pews. Talented locals also carved statues, made wrought iron light fittings and created the terracotta and slipware Stations of the Cross. Light, colourful, warm and welcoming, St Kyneburgha's feels a much loved and cared for parish church.

– IRELAND –

ST PATRICK'S CATHEDRAL, DUBLIN

For a country considered to be Catholic, visitors are often surprised to discover that the biggest church in Ireland and its national cathedral is Protestant and belongs to the Church of Ireland. In fact Dublin has two Church of Ireland cathedrals, St Patrick's and Christ Church, and there's a fair amount of history between them.

Ireland's legendary patron saint, St Patrick, was in his teens in the 5th century when he was captured by Irish raiders and taken as a slave to County Antrim. After six years he escaped to Gaul where he studied, was ordained and later made a Bishop. Believing he was called by God to return to Ireland, he spent the rest of his life travelling throughout the country, converting people to Christianity and founding many churches. On one of his visits to Dublin, it's believed that he baptised converts at a well beside the River Poddle (which still runs beneath Patrick Street) outside the old city walls. A small wooden church was erected close by to mark the event.

This was the site chosen by Archbishop John Comyn to build his church. It was dedicated to God, Our Blessed Lady Mary and St Patrick on St Patrick's Day (17 March) 1192.

Christ Church Cathedral was already in existence when Cormyn arrived in Dublin from England, and well known for its popular, reforming and recently deceased Irish Archbishop, Laurence O'Toole (who was later canonised and became a patron saint of the city). However, it was a monastic foundation, and having been sent by King Henry

II to re-organise the Irish church, the Anglo-Norman Comyn was not happy about living in the palace beside the Augustinian priory church or being subject to the municipal jurisdiction of the City Provosts.

Upsetting the locals wasn't part of his remit, so he erected his own palace and secular church outside the city walls, where he could exercise complete control. It became a collegiate church, dedicated to education and scholarship, and then elevated to cathedral status, as befitted an archbishop. However a successor, Archbishop Luke, considered Comyn's building too small and rebuilt it on a much loftier scale, cruciform in shape, in the Early English Gothic style. It was rededicated in 1254 with the Lady Chapel added in about 1270. Together they form the basis of today's cathedral.

Dublin's two cathedrals, less than half a mile apart, had a confrontational existence. In 1300 some of their disputes were resolved by a Papal decree, *Pacis Composito*, which clearly defined the role of each one. While their shared status was acknowledged, Christ Church was to be the senior cathedral of the diocese, where the consecration and enthronement of the Archbishop of Dublin should take place.

Technically, then, St Patrick's is not a cathedral as it doesn't contain the Bishop's Chair, but it was too big and impressive to be downgraded to a parish church and was allowed to keep its designation. When in 1869, the Irish Church Act disestablished the Church of Ireland as the state Church, St Patrick's became the National Cathedral for the Church of Ireland while Christ Church became the local cathedral for the diocese of Dublin and Glendalough.

Down the centuries St Patrick's has been through many changes: built and rebuilt, repaired after storm, fire and flooding, stripped of its finery during the Reformation, demoted to parish church and used as a courthouse under

King Edward VI, restored to cathedral status under the Catholic Queen Mary, then returned four years later to Anglicanism under Queen Elizabeth I.

In 1651, during the English Civil War, Oliver Cromwell used it for courts-martial. In 1688, King James II and his fellow Catholics briefly repossessed St Patrick's but after his defeat by the Protestant King William III of England (William of Orange) at the Battle of the Boyne in 1690, the cathedral reverted once more to Anglicanism. A chair reputed to have been used by King William at a service of celebration after the battle is on display in the north choir aisle.

The chequered history had deleterious effects on the fabric of the building. While several major attempts had been made at restoration, by the start of the 19th century the cathedral was in such a dire state that it was considered in danger of collapse. In 1860, in stepped Benjamin Lee Guinness of the brewing dynasty with an offer to pay for the cathedral's rebuilding, the only proviso being that he could get on with the work without interference. Five years on, the cathedral reopened with a new ceiling on the nave and none of the screens that had previously separated the nave, choir and transepts.

Restoration of the interior continued for some years, with Benjamin Lee's sons adding the beautifully coloured floor tiles, their intricate patterns based on medieval designs. They bring striking life and vibrancy to the building.

The central aisle of the soaring, three-tiered nave offers a fine view up past the carved choir stalls to the high altar. The two side aisles are lined with statues and memorial plaques. Behind the high altar, the Lady Chapel with its slender columns of dark grey stone was beautifully restored in 2013.

There's no medieval stained glass here, all the windows date from the 19th and 20th centuries and tell many stories.

St Patrick's window at the west end offers 39 different episodes in the saint's life. There are windows celebrating the philanthropist Guinness family, including one in memory of Annie Lee Plunkett, daughter of Benjamin Lee Guinness (and wife of Archbishop Plunkett). Renowned for her charitable works, the Bible quotation chosen for her window – 'I was thirsty and ye gave me drink' – seems apt, given her family connections. In the north transept, windows commemorate three different wars: the First World War, in which up to 50,000 Irish citizens died, the Crimean War and the South African War.

Regimental colours hang from walls and war memorials feature heavily among the over 200 monuments in the cathedral, which include those to former archbishops, deans, politicians and writers. The most famous of St Patrick's deans is Jonathan Swift, author of *Gulliver's Travels*. He was Dean of St Patrick's Cathedral from 1713 until his death in 1745 and fought hard against social injustice. He is buried in the cathedral and as well as his death masks, many artefacts associated with his life are on display.

For the First World War centenary in 2014, the cathedral's first new war monument in 50 years was unveiled in the north transept. Made from steel and suitably 'broken', its base surrounded by barbed wire – the universal symbol of conflict – the Tree of Remembrance is to honour all those who have been afflicted by conflict, anywhere in the world.

Music has played an integral part in cathedral life ever since the choir school was formed in 1432, the oldest school in Ireland. In 1742 the combined choirs of St Patrick's and Christ Church sang the first performance of Handel's *Messiah*, not in the cathedral but in a music hall theatre.

Just beside the cathedral, in the Cathedral Close, you'll find the wonderful and unmissable Marsh's Library.

Photo: Steven Lek

Founded by Archbishop Narcissus Marsh as the first public library in Ireland, the interior with its beautiful dark oak bookcases has remained largely unchanged since it was built in the early 18th century.

A magnificent example of an Early Enlightenment library, it houses over 25,000 rare books and manuscripts from the 15th to the 18th centuries. Many of its collections are still kept on the shelves allocated to them by the archbishop and the first librarian, a scholar and French Huguenot refugee, Dr Elias Bouhéreau.

The saying 'to chance your arm' had its origins at St Patrick's. In 1492, two powerful Irish families, the Butlers and the FitzGeralds, were engaged in a bitter feud. During a fierce battle, the Butlers took refuge in the Chapter House of the Cathedral and refused to emerge when a truce was offered. Gerald FitzGerald hacked a hole in the door and thrust his arm through it, offering his hand to the Butlers on the other side. Having risked (or chanced) his arm, it was assumed he was serious, so hands were shaken and peace made. The Door of Reconciliation can be seen in the cathedral's north transept.

– SCOTLAND –

ST MAGNUS CATHEDRAL, KIRKWALL

Uniquely, Britain's most northerly cathedral belongs not to the Church but to the people of Orkney. King James III of Scotland assigned its ownership to the city and community of Kirkwall in 1486, the year he elevated Kirkwall to the status of a royal burgh.

The Orkney Islands lie 19 kilometres (12 miles) off the north coast of Scotland, across the storm-swept Pentland Firth. Kirkwall, their capital and the principal town on the largest of the islands, known as the Mainland, grew out of a former Viking settlement and trading post. Probably founded in the 11th century, when the islands were under Norse rule, its name is derived from the Old Norse word *Kirkjuvagr*, meaning Church of the Bay.

Built with warm red sandstone and known as the 'Light in the North', St Magnus Cathedral dominates Kirkwall's skyline. It is a glorious example of Romanesque architecture and the best-preserved medieval cathedral in Scotland.

At the suggestion of his father, Kol, who supervised the initial building work, Earl Rögnvald founded the cathedral in memory of his uncle, the popular Earl Magnus. Murdered, (martyred, it is said), by his cousin and rival on the island of Egilsay where they'd met to resolve a dispute, he was canonised in 1135. When his bones were returned to Kirkwall and placed in a shrine, it became a place of pilgrimage and miracles were believed to have taken place there. The construction that had begun in 1137 continued for some 300 years.

The massive Norman pillars in the nave are reminiscent of those in Durham Cathedral (page 29) and indeed the original design for St Magnus was heavily influenced by that of Durham. The death of Earl Rögnvald in the 1150s brought construction to a standstill. A new, much larger plan had been envisaged by the time building restarted around 1190 and, given several extensions, it would take until the 15th century before it was completed.

Much of its warmth and appeal comes from the use of

Photo: WKnight94

local red sandstone combined with yellow ochre sandstone for decorative effect. St Magnus may not be as big as the great English cathedrals, but its unity of style and the fine proportions of its graceful yet solid structure give it a sense of size that belies its actual dimensions.

Its interior is uncluttered, very much a place for worship, but there are several notable monuments to see and some good stained glass. There are memorials to two 19th-century Orcadian explorers, Dr John Rae, who charted much of the Canadian Arctic but never received the honours he deserved, and to the missionary William Balfour Baikie who navigated up the Niger River and translated parts of the Bible into Hausa. The writer Eric Linklater spent many years in Orkney, identifying strongly with the islands of his father's birth. He is remembered here, as is the great Stromness poet, George Mackay Brown.

Perhaps because it was under local ownership – maybe it was more difficult to desecrate the property of councillors, magistrates and the Kirkwall community – St Magnus didn't suffer as badly as most cathedrals in 1560 during the Reformation, although the organ, treasures and rich vestments were removed and the wall decorations covered in whitewash. A hundred years later, the building was damaged during Oliver Cromwell's siege when the Roundheads used the cathedral as a barracks and for stabling.

In the mid-19th century, the cathedral was in a very poor state of repair and major building restoration took place, but by the early 20th century it was again in bad shape. Thanks to a considerable bequest from Sheriff Thoms, who is commemorated in the fine east window, substantial renovations were carried out between 1919 and 1930.

Work included replacing the slated pyramid roof atop the bell tower with a tall copper spire, the original having been struck by lightning in 1671; installing stained glass in the previously plain glass windows and laying floor tiles based on medieval designs. It was at this time that the relics of St Magnus were discovered in a pillar in the choir. Rögnvald's relics, discovered at an earlier date, are in a pillar opposite. Finally the wonderful warm pink sandstone was again revealed, emerging from beneath layers of plaster and whitewash.

The east end of the choir was dedicated as St Rögnvald's Chapel in 1965. Carved figures representing Kol, Earl Rögnvald and Kirkwall's first Bishop, Bishop William, were designed by the Kirkwall-born artist, Sir Stanley Cursiter.

The brilliant west window by Scottish stained glass artist, Crear McCartney, is considered one of the finest contemporary windows in Scotland. Commissioned for the cathedral's 850th anniversary in 1987, it was entirely paid for by public subscription.

As well as hosting concerts and recitals throughout the year, the cathedral is a major venue for the St Magnus International Festival, a midsummer (June) celebration of the arts featuring world-class performances.

Next to the cathedral are the ruins of the former Bishop's Palace (12th century) and the Renaissance-style Earl's Palace. Don't miss the exhibits in the Orkney Museum across the way in historic Tankerness House, once a manse for cathedral clergy.

– WALES –

ST DAVIDS CATHEDRAL, PEMBROKESHIRE

Most British cathedrals are in the centre of a city or, like those in Durham (page 29) and Lincoln (page 24), stand high above the townscape at their feet. St Davids, however, snuggles into a valley. The approach from town through the 14th-century Tower Gate is much higher than the cathedral so, rather unexpectedly, your first sight of the dusky pink sandstone building is a bird's-eye view of its roofs.

In the 6th century, St David (Dewi Sant), Wales' patron saint, founded a monastery and church here, hidden away among dense bushes and trees in a boggy valley by the River Alun. Stories of the monks' ascetic lives of prayer, study and hard labour in the fields attracted pilgrims but their location near the Pembrokeshire coast, on the sea route to Ireland, also attracted the unwanted attention of passing Vikings, raiders and pirates.

The monastery became a renowned religious and intellectual centre, but down the centuries raiders murdered at least two of its bishops and by 1089 St David's shrine had been vandalised and stripped of the precious metals that adorned it.

William the Conqueror came here to pray in 1081, though he may have been more interested in its strategic peninsula position and proximity to Ireland. The Normans saw the Celtic religion as inferior to their own and the Welsh church as a threat to their controlling rule, therefore in need of reform.

In 1115, King Henry I appointed Bernard as the first Norman bishop of St Davids. He began building a new cathedral, dedicated in 1131, and shrewdly persuaded the Pope to make St Davids a place of pilgrimage: two journeys to St Davids were equivalent to one to Rome. That church was rebuilt in the Transitional Norman style in the 1180s and forms the basis of the cathedral today.

The light that floods the 12th-century nave highlights the warm colours of the stone arcade, its alternate round and octagonal piers supporting wide, decoratively carved, Romanesque arches.

The nave's oak ceiling is one of the cathedral's glories. It dates from the early 16th century and is a wonder of exquisite carving, with arches and pendants belying the fact that it is actually flat, suspended from tie beams. Medieval motifs appear in the lace-like detail, along with Renaissance features of dragon-shaped dolphins.

From the back of the nave you can see how the walls lean outwards and the sloping floor means that here you, quite literally, walk up the aisle.

The delicately carved stone pulpitum that separates the nave from the choir was the work of Bishop Henry Gower, who made substantial changes to the building and its surroundings during his tenure from 1328 to 1347. His tomb is housed within the screen, alongside a statue of St David dressed as a medieval bishop.

It was Bishop Gower who built the huge Bishop's Palace that broods nearby. Its still impressive ruins, richly embellished with stone carvings and arcaded parapets, speak of the wealth and power of the church in the 14th century.

One of the stalls in the magnificent choir bears the royal coat of arms – uniquely, the reigning British sovereign is a member of the cathedral chapter. The misericords hidden

Photo: Nilfanion

under the 16th-century seats suggest a mischievous streak in their carvers. Among the faces and mythical beasts, one depicts seasick pilgrims in a boat, another a man with backache. Look up: the tower lantern ceiling is beautiful.

Of the chapels beyond the choir, Holy Trinity has fine fan vaulting, an altar pieced together from medieval fragments and in the original pilgrims' recess, a casket many believed held the bones of St David and St Justinian.

In 1536 during the Reformation, the strongly Protestant Bishop William Barker ripped out St David's shrine, stripping it of its jewels and relics. The tomb of Edmund Tudor, King Henry VII's father, was moved here after the dissolution of the monastery at Carmarthen and placed in front of the high altar. A century later, Oliver Cromwell's troops did serious damage to the building, stripping the roofs of lead, wrecking the medieval library, smashing stained glass windows and tearing up tomb brasses.

Restoration work occurred in the 18th century but it was Sir George Gilbert Scott, the prolific English Gothic revival architect, who made a major contribution to the look and stability of the cathedral towards the end of the 19th century. Further restoration continued on through the 20th century, including the addition of some fine stained glass.

St David's shrine, visited by many thousands of pilgrims until it was destroyed in the Reformation, has been beautifully restored and was rededicated on St David's Day, 1 March, 2012. Painted and gilded icons of St David and fellow saints sit within the shrine's original niches. The oak canopy above it, painted in medieval colours, replicates that of the 13th-century construction.

It breathes history, but St Davids Cathedral is very much a 21st-century church. Its choir is unique in the United Kingdom in that the top line of the full choir is sung by girl choristers aged eight to eighteen. It is also the seat of the first woman bishop to be elected by the Church in Wales.

Visitors speak of a palpable sense of serenity and spirituality in this cathedral within the Pembrokeshire Coast National Park on the far south-west coast of Wales. The town of St Davids has city status but in reality is hardly bigger than a village. Its narrow streets can get very crowded during the summer months and especially during St Davids Cathedral Festival, a feast of classical and contemporary music concerts held annually at the end of May.

EUROPE

– AUSTRIA –

ST STEPHEN'S CATHEDRAL, VIENNA

Symbol of Vienna, beloved by its residents, the Stephansdom stands at the geographic centre and emotional heart of the city. Piercing the skyline and standing 137 metres (450 feet) tall, the slim south tower, all delicate stonework and affectionately known as the Steffl, was 65 years in the making. The steeply sloping, boldly patterned roof, created from over 200,000 glazed tiles, has become a favourite local landmark.

In a city better known for its Baroque grandeur, St Stephen's is a Gothic masterpiece. Building was initiated in 1359 when the Habsburg Duke Rudolf IV laid the foundation stone of the Gothic nave. Incorporating features from its two 12th- and 13th-century Romanesque predecessors, it took over 200 years to complete and encompasses detail from the medieval era to the Baroque.

The main entrance is the oldest part of the building. Birds, lions, dragons, monks, winged sirens, dogs and demons decorate the massive Giant's Door (Riesentor), which is topped with a tympanum of Christ in Majesty, resting on a rainbow and flanked by winged angels. Both the entrance and the two 65-metre (213-foot)-high cream-coloured bell towers (Heldentürm) above it are Romanesque and date from the 13th century.

Look for the O5 carved into the stone by the door. As the number 5 refers to E, the fifth letter of the alphabet and OE is the abbreviation for Österreich (Austria), it was a covert sign of resistance during the Nazi annexation of the country.

Two side doors in the High Gothic style from the 1370s – the Bishop's Gate once used as the entrance reserved for women and the Singer Gate, the men's entrance – have finely carved tympanums depicting the Coronation of the Virgin and the life and conversion of St Paul.

The interior is dark and atmospheric, but never gloomy. St Stephen's is a hall-church – a vast nave with two side aisles of almost equal height and width ending with three apses – the blueprint for many Austrian churches of later date. They soar on statue-adorned pillars and piers to elegant lierne vaulting high above. Light enters from tall windows in the aisles and apses.

Presiding over the nave, the stone pulpit (c.1500) is a whirl of decorative sculpture. From a web of intricate detail and supporting saints, relief portraits of St Augustine of Hippo, St Ambrose, St Gregory the Great and St Jerome (the four Doctors of the Church), depicted in different temperaments and stages of life, seemingly peer out from stone windows.

A sweeping staircase curves, sinuously, around the supporting pillar. On its handrail, three-leafed wheels representing the Holy Trinity point upwards, four-leafed wheels representing the seasons as worldly life point downwards, lizards and toads fight a battle of good over evil and a dog at the top protects the preacher. Tucked below the stairs, the master mason has left us a portrait of himself.

Ahead, the marble and stone high altar is mid-17th century Baroque and took seven years to build. Flanked by statues of local saints, a large painting shows the stoning of St Stephen. In a panel above, Christ is welcoming St Stephen, the first Christian martyr, into heaven. Behind the altar, the apse's three stunning stained glass windows add further brilliance.

There are numerous altars in the cathedral but the must-see is the four-winged Wiener Neustädter altarpiece dating from 1447, which stands to the left of the high altar. Painted panels of saints open out to reveal carved scenes from the life of the Virgin Mary and her child, the figures beautifully defined and gilded. Its restoration began in 1985, involved ten art restorers and took twenty years to complete.

The ornate, red marble tomb of Emperor Friedrich III stands in state in the chancel to the right of the high altar. An extraordinary work of art, 45 years in the making, the sarcophagus shows Frederick in his coronation robes surrounded by the coats of arms of all his dominions and contains 240 carved statues. It was under his rule that in 1469 the city became a bishopric and St Stephen's the mother church in the newly formed Diocese of Vienna. In 1722, Pope Innocent XIII elevated it to an archbishopric.

Among the various chapels, stop at St Catherine's to

Photo: Jakub Hałun

look at the fourteen-sided baptismal font. Dating from the 15th century, the four evangelists are depicted on its base and marble niches feature the twelve Apostles, Christ and St Stephen.

The chapel is at the foot of the south tower (the Steffl) that, if you have the energy, you can climb. Choose a good-weather day and your reward for conquering the 343 steeply winding steps of the tight spiral staircase to the watch room – used as an observation and command post during the Siege of Vienna in 1529, the Battle of Vienna in 1683 and for fire-watching duty up to 1955 – will be fabulous views of the city and way beyond.

The original intention had been for the north tower to match it in height but by 1511, when building was halted, it was a 'mere' 68 metres (223 feet). It was given its ill-considered Renaissance cap about 65 years later. The north tower may not be as tall or impressive as the south, but it has a fast elevator and the views from the platform are pretty good.

This tower houses the gigantic Pummerin (or Boomer) Bell, which traditionally rings in the New Year across the city and out to the entire country. The original bell was cast from captured Turkish cannons in the 17th century. After it crashed down through the roof during a disastrous fire in 1945, it was replaced by an even larger, twenty-tonne version, incorporating fragments of the old.

From tower level you can get a closer look at the colourful roof, patterned with diamonds, zigzags, the Habsburg double-headed eagle and the coats of arms of the City of Vienna and the Republic of Austria. Nearly a quarter-of-a-million glazed tiles were needed to create it and the date of its completion, 1950, is up there too.

It's hard to imagine that much of St Stephen's was reduced

to rubble after a fire caught hold towards the very end of the Second World War, bringing the roof crashing down into the nave. Many treasures were saved but the 15th-century carved choir stalls burned. The rebuilding that started immediately was completed in 1952.

Music plays an important role at St Stephen's, as it has always done, and many a famous composer has been connected with the cathedral. When Wolfgang Amadeus Mozart lived in nearby Domgasse (where he wrote *The Marriage of Figaro*) it would have been his local parish church. He was married to Constanze Weber here, two of his children were baptised in St Catherine's Chapel and his funeral in 1791 was held in the Chapel of the Cross.

Discovered by the then director of music, the eight-year-old Joseph Haydn came to Vienna as a choirboy and remained a chorister at St Stephen's for nine years. He was a choirboy when the funeral of Antonio Vivaldi took place in 1741. In 1760 Haydn married Maria Anna Keller in the Eligius Chapel. It's said that it was only when Beethoven realised he couldn't hear the ringing of the cathedral's bells that he became aware of the full extent of his deafness.

The main part of the cathedral closes at the end of the day, but the back section by the main entrance is open to visit until 10 pm. Here, banks of flickering candles in front of the (believed to be miracle-working) Maria Pötsch icon of the Madonna and Child reflect its importance to the constant flow of people who visit it for a few minutes of silent prayer. With the darkened church in the background, it's a very atmospheric place to be.

SALZBURG CATHEDRAL, SALZBURG

Dedicated to its founding fathers and local patron saints, St Rupert and St Vergil, Salzburg's monumental cathedral (Dom) with its magnificent marble façade and mighty copper-green dome is considered the finest Early Baroque building north of the Alps.

Three mighty bronze doors bear the symbols of faith, love and hope and, seemingly guarding them, four colossal marble statues depict Saints Peter and Paul, bearing respectively a golden key and a sword, and Rupert and Vergil with a salt barrel and a model church. Look up to see the Four Evangelists: Matthew, Mark, Luke and John, and on the pediment, Christ flanked by Moses and Elijah. Twin towers rise up 79 metres (260 feet) alongside them.

The numbers displayed on the wrought iron gates tell of the years when the cathedral was consecrated: 774, 1628 and 1959.

The first bishop, the 8th-century missionary St Rupert, came to the ruined Roman town of Juvavum, made it his base and renamed it Salzburg, possibly for the salt that made the area's fortune or in reference to its location on the Salzach River. Already a site of early Christianity, he laid the foundations of his cathedral, which, when he died in around 710, was finished by his successor, the Irish-born Bishop Vergilius (St Vergil). It was consecrated in 774.

Throughout the Middle Ages came renovations and rebuilding, lightning strikes and fires, construction and reconstruction, ending in a very fine, very large, five-aisled Romanesque basilica. A fire in 1598 wrought so much damage that the ambitious Prince-Archbishop Wolf Dietrich von Raitenau ordered its demolition, with a new cathedral to be built in the latest Italian Baroque style.

Building work started under his successor, Prince-Archbishop Markus Sittikus von Hohenems, the cathedral was designed by Italian architect Santino Solari and consecrated in 1628 by Archbishop Paris Lodron to the sound of twelve choirs singing a *Te Deum* composed by the Kapellmeister to the Salzburg court.

In 1944, the dome and parts of the sanctuary were destroyed during an Allied bombing attack. After fifteen years of restoration work, the cathedral was re-consecrated in 1959.

Stepping inside the cathedral, which can accommodate thousands of worshippers, the nave appears quite dark. A feeling of calm pervades the predominantly sepia and white colouring that features throughout the building.

Phenomenal stuccowork, outlined in black and effectively defining the intricate detail, decorates arches, pillars and galleries. Elaborately framed frescoes depicting the Life and Passion of Christ bring warm colour to the barrel-vaulted ceiling.

The darkness draws your eye towards the 17th-century painting of the Resurrection of Christ on the high altar. In this eastern part of the cathedral, three semi-circular apses are linked, clover-like, beneath the mighty dome. Here light streams in from the 71-metre (233-foot)-high octagonal cupola, falling on dizzying frescoes, trompe-l'oeil vistas and an intensity of stone carving. Encircling the altar are four organs and music balconies that can accommodate up to 50 musicians and solo voices.

There are no side aisles, but between the massive double pilasters on either side of the nave, arches open into small chapels, each with its altar and all decorated with stucco. The

Image: Wikiolo

chapel to the left of the entrance houses a Romanesque font from 1321. In bronze, sitting on lions' paws and decorated with reliefs of saints, it is where Mozart was baptised, as was Joseph Mohr who wrote the Christmas carol *Silent Night*.

At the time Wolfgang Amadeus was growing up, Salzburg was one of the most renowned intellectual and cultural cities in Europe. As Konzertmeister at the Prince-Archbishop's court he wrote much sacred music, including the *Coronation Mass*, the best known of his complete Masses, and played the huge main organ at the west end of the cathedral.

You can get up close to this majestic organ, surrounded by carved angels playing instruments and crowned by golden statues of St Rupert and St Vergil, on a visit to the Cathedral Museum, which features treasures spanning 1,300 years. You'll also get the best view of the cathedral from up there in the organ loft.

Salzburg Cathedral is famous for its music – even the most secular of music-loving visitors head here for High Mass on Sunday – and a concert here is a treat.

Outside, the Domplatz, with a Marian column at its centre, is the setting for performances of *Jederman* (*Everyman*), the morality play that has featured in the prestigious Salzburg Festival every year since 1920. During the popular Advent market, musicians and singers crowd onto the cathedral's steps for impromptu concerts.

Mozart's sister Nannerl is buried nearby in the beautiful cemetery attached to the Stiftskirche St Peter. This magnificent church, founded as an abbey by St Rupert, has Romanesque and Gothic cloisters, a spectacular Rococo interior and is well worth visiting.

– BELGIUM –

CATHEDRAL OF OUR LADY, ANTWERP

Belgium's largest church, and arguably the loveliest, Onze-Lieve-Vrouwekathedraal attracts visitors for the four magnificent paintings by Peter Paul Rubens – but with its sweeping Gothic lines and soaring vaults, it has much to impress in its own right.

The spire is spectacular. Gracefully tiered and towering to a height of 123 metres (404 feet), it is a wonder of delicate, filigree lace-like stonework. Rising above the historic heart of the city – an Old Town of narrow cobbled streets, pedestrian lanes, crooked houses and Baroque churches – it watches over the step-gabled guild houses and ornate Town Hall in the Grote Markt, Antwerp's most famous square.

Begun in 1352 and completed by around 1520, the cathedral was preceded by a 10th-century chapel and a 12th-century Romanesque church. The choir and nave were built first, between 1352 and 1411, the west front followed between 1422 and 1474, with the octagonal north tower constructed between 1501 and 1507. The spire was added between 1502 and 1518. Originally, two towers of equal height were envisaged, but the south tower was never completed and remains at roughly half the intended height.

Tympanum sculptures above the main door depict the Last Judgement. Inside, the cathedral boasts seven aisles, 125 pillars and 128 windows (55 of them with vibrant stained glass). Three aisles flank each side of the long central nave, their graceful medieval ribbed vaults bestowing a sense of lightness and great height to the church.

The design of this huge, gleaming white space, which comfortably seats 2,400 worshippers, reflects the city's tumultuous history.

During the rise of Protestantism across Europe, between 1566 and 1581, Calvinists looted and badly damaged the Gothic interior. It was restored in the Baroque style and local artist Peter Paul Rubens provided paintings for the by then bare walls. During the French Revolution two centuries later, the building was threatened with demolition. It survived, but most of the contents were sold or appropriated. This time it was restored and redesigned in the neo-Gothic style.

Despite all the plundering, some major art treasures survived. They include medieval wall paintings and the 15th-century bronze effigy of Isabella of Bourbon, hands in prayer and accompanied by her pet dog. The highlights, though, are four masterworks by Rubens.

Seeing the massive canvases of *The Raising of the Cross* and *The Descent from the Cross* for the first time leaves the viewer in silent awe. The powerful, larger than life-size figures in the centre panels are intense and dramatic and you can feel every stretched sinew as they struggle to raise the cross and bear the weight of Christ's body.

Rubens painted them soon after he had returned from eight years working in Italy and stylistically was clearly influenced by artists such as Caravaggio and Michelangelo.

The triptych of *The Raising of the Cross*, completed in 1609–10, is 4.6 metres (15 feet) high and 6.4 metres (21 feet) wide when open. The left side panel shows the grieving Virgin Mary and St John the Evangelist; the right panel has Roman soldiers preparing the two thieves for their crucifixion alongside Christ. Saints associated with (the since demolished) St Walburga's Church in Antwerp, where the work was originally installed, are depicted on the exterior of the wings.

In the 4.2- by 3.2-metre (14- by 10-foot) main panel of *The Descent from the Cross*, St John, clothed in fiery red, helps steady Christ's broken body. Painted between 1611 and 1614, Rubens' use of light against darkness has great impact. Side panels depict the Visitation of Mary to her cousin Elizabeth and the Presentation of Jesus at the Temple.

In 1794, Napoleon removed both works to The Louvre in Paris. They were returned to Antwerp in 1816 after his defeat, to the sound of church bells ringing out their 'welcome home'. Today they stand within the transept's outstretched arms.

High, high above, in the crossing tower, the perspective in the huge circular painting of *The Assumption of the Virgin* by the 17th-century artist Cornelis Schut is such that the tower appears to extend into infinity. Look for the stunning silver frontage on the central altar of the crossing. Its intricate design incorporates acanthus leaves and roses around a depiction of the Virgin Mary's birth.

Beyond the monumental, neo-Gothic, carved wood choir stalls – which were 40 years in the making – is the high altar and, framed by marble columns, another work of genius.

Rubens painted *The Assumption of the Virgin Mary* as an altarpiece for the cathedral in 1626. Full of colour and movement, it shows the twelve Apostles and the three women who, according to legend, were present at Mary's death, looking on in awe as a cloud of playful cherubs lift the Virgin towards a burst of divine light.

In a chapel to the right of the choir look for *The Resurrection of Christ* triptych. Rubens painted this for Martina Plantin, widow of the printer Jan Moretus, in 1611–12. In the main

panel, Christ strides triumphant and radiant from his open rock tomb as astounded Roman soldiers cower at his feet. The side panels depict the couple's patron saints: John the Baptist and St Martina.

On the left of the choir, seek out St Joseph's Chapel for the very fine St Joseph retable. Although created in the late 19th century, it has a medieval feel. With paintings on the side panels, the finely carved figures in the centre tell of seven episodes in Joseph's life.

Two standout images of the Virgin Mary are situated in the north aisle's Mary Chapel. At its entrance there's an exquisite 14th-century statue of a serene Mother Mary gently holding her infant son, Jesus. It is carved from Carrara marble. Inside the large, heavily decorated chapel, the regally dressed Our Lady of Antwerp from the 16th century is the most revered statue in the cathedral.

In the south aisle's Sacrament Chapel, the highlight is a Rococo tabernacle in the form of the Ark of the Covenant, gilded and decorated with chased reliefs by Antwerp gold- and silversmiths.

At the heart of the nave, a parrot, a crane and a small owl are among the birds and small animals that make their homes among the trees and vegetation of the richly carved, 18th-century oak pulpit. Saints and Rococo cherubs have their place too; four female figures embody the continents of Europe, Asia, America and Africa, the Holy Spirit appears as a white dove with outstretched wings and above them all, an angel trumpets the good news. It has been said that the pulpit contains more meaning than some sermons!

From the tower, a carillon of 49 bells rings out across town on summer Sunday afternoons. Climb its 500 steps for views that can extend as far as Brussels on a clear day.

– CZECH REPUBLIC –

ST VITUS CATHEDRAL, PRAGUE

High on its hill, watching over the Vltava River and dominating the skyline wherever you are in the city, Prague's great Gothic cathedral took 600 years to complete and is the spiritual symbol of the whole Czech nation.

At the heart of the Prague Castle complex, the King of Bohemia (and soon to be Holy Roman Emperor) Charles IV laid the foundations for a suitably grand cathedral when Prague became an archbishopric in 1344. It had previously been the site of a rotunda church founded by St Wenceslas in 925, which held a relic of the young Sicilian martyr, St Vitus, and an 11th-century Romanesque basilica.

Wars, iconoclasm, fires and the complications of history intervened until the cathedral was finally consecrated in 1929, though the decoration still wasn't completed by then. Originally dedicated solely to St Vitus, since 1997 it has been known officially as The Metropolitan Cathedral of Saints Vitus, Wenceslas and Adalbert – three of Bohemia's patron saints to whom the 11th-century church was dedicated.

There's a delicate beauty about the vast interior and, perhaps surprisingly given the length of time of building and intervening architectural styles, a harmonious sense of unity. Gothic and Neo-Gothic combine so well it's hard to see the joins. With most of Prague's numerous superb churches being heavily Baroque, St Vitus stands out from the crowd in more than just size.

Charles IV envisaged Bohemia as one of the most powerful

nations in the medieval world, as indeed it went on to be, and a great cathedral was required as a suitable setting for the coronation of future kings.

For this he called on the best architects and summoned Matthias of Arras from the papal palace at Avignon. His French Gothic influence can be detected in some of the chapels. After his death, the Swabian mason, sculptor and architect Peter Parler took over as principal architect in 1356, at the age of only 23.

One of the most influential craftsmen of the Middle Ages, Parler also built the Charles Bridge and much of Prague's New Town (Nové Mesto). Unfortunately for the cathedral, the king kept him so busy with other work, including churches all over the realm, that by the time he died in 1397 only the magnificent chancel and parts of the transept had been finished. Two of his sons, his nephew and members of Parler's workshop continued building, but came to an abrupt stop with the outbreak of the Hussite Wars in 1419.

Above the arcades of the soaring, three-aisled nave, where massive piers reach to stylish vaulting, a gallery runs the length of the cathedral. Huge stained glass windows rise to roof height and the light falling through their rich, intense colours creates playful patterns on stone. Created in the 20th century, they are vibrant modern masterpieces.

In the choir, the Royal Oratory, an immense imperial mausoleum three tombs wide, stands behind splendid 16th-century wrought iron gates. Opposite it, steps lead down into the Royal Crypt, where several members of Bohemian royalty are buried, including Charles IV, who died in 1378. Visible along the way are vestiges of the old Romanesque basilica and original rotunda church.

Wherever you look it seems there are tombs of saints and

archbishops, kings, princes, dukes and rulers, especially in the numerous side aisle chapels, many containing fine works of art.

Visit the third chapel on the left as you enter through the west portal, to view the distinctive Art Nouveau design in the window painted by Czech artist Alphons Mucha. It depicts the legendary lives and work of Slav missionaries, Saints Cyril and Methodius.

The elaborate tomb of the much-revered Czech martyr, St John Nepomuk, crafted from solid silver in the 18th century, stands in the ambulatory to the right of the main altar. Bearing a crucifix, the saint kneels on his tomb under a canopy, the fringes of its curtains held by flying angels that were donated by the Empress Maria Theresa. The whole is a masterpiece of the silversmiths' art.

At the ancient core of the cathedral, Peter Parler's 14th-century St Wenceslas Chapel, is magnificent. Glorious Gothic frescoes showing scenes from Christ's Passion and the life of the saintly Bohemian duke (he was posthumously declared to be a king) cover the walls. They are interspersed with gilt-set slabs of semi-precious stones, over 1,300 of them, mainly jasper, turquoise and amethyst. St Wenceslas' tomb, in the shape of an ark, is draped in red and gold cloth.

At the back of the chapel, the Bohemian crown jewels lie behind a door with seven locks. The President of the Czech Republic is one of the seven people to hold a key.

St Wenceslas is an important figure in Czech history. Although only 28 when he died – murdered by his younger brother in a church in 935 – he brought Christianity to the people and is the patron saint of the Czech Republic. His feast day, 28 September, is a national holiday: Day of the Czech Statehood.

Outside the cathedral, admire the spires and flying

Photo: Lynx1211

buttresses and don't miss the ceremonial south entrance known as the Golden Portal. Its *Last Judgement* mosaic dates from the 1370s. Made from over a million Bohemian glass and stone tesserae, its centrepiece depicts Christ in Glory above Czech saints and the kneeling Charles IV and his wife Elizabeth of Pomerania. The dead rising from their tombs, assisted by angels, are seen on the left, with Satan overseeing hellfire on the right.

The Neo-Gothic west front with its two spires is the newest part of the cathedral, built in the late 19th and early 20th centuries. Reliefs on the bronze door at the main entrance show scenes from the history of the cathedral and legends about St Wenceslas and St Adalbert. The rose window above, fashioned in 1925, depicts Biblical stories of Creation.

The Bell Tower, begun by Peter Parler in the 14th century and containing the massive eighteen-tonne bell Zikmund, can be climbed in good weather. The 287 narrow, winding steps spiral up to a viewing platform and panoramic, bird's-eye views over Prague.

– FINLAND –

TEMPPELIAUKIO CHURCH, HELSINKI

One of the most innovative and best loved of modern churches, the Rock Church, surrounded by apartments in a residential square of the Töölo district of Helsinki, gets its name because it is, literally, embedded inside solid rock. Its walls are rough granite, its dome is lined with copper and an ice-age crevice serves as an altarpiece. The church was consecrated in 1969.

Looked at from above, a bird's-eye perspective might suggest that a flying saucer had sunk into the ground where it landed. Approaching from street level, it's as if one is entering a cave, the uninviting concrete at the entrance more like that of an underground car park than a church. But inside it is brilliant in its simplicity and atmosphere.

This ingenious construction was designed by architect brothers Timo and Tuomo Suomalainen, winners of the third competition held to build a church at this location.

The first was back in 1932 when the district was being made into an independent parish. The judges weren't impressed with the entries and launched a second competition four years later. This time a winning plan was announced but it didn't get very far before being shelved at the outbreak of the Second World War. In 1961 a new competition was announced.

In the winning proposal from the Suomalainen brothers, the bedrock was to be kept as intact as possible by embedding the church within it and placing the other parish facilities on the edges of the mound.

It wasn't a popular decision. Locals wanted a more conventional and traditional church and newspaper reports about the design were disparaging. A group of Christian students thought that the money could be better spent helping Biafran victims of the famine that followed their devastating struggle for independence from Nigeria. To make their point, they painted the word Biafra around the area and over the church foundations. It was the first graffiti in Finland.

Building continued, despite all the attempts to get it stopped, but local attitudes softened after its completion

Photo: MKFI

in 1969. By the early 1970s congregations were filling the church for the Lutheran services and it was receiving over 100,000 visitors. Today the annual visitor numbers are over half a million.

Within its free-form oval shape, the 24-metre (79-foot)-diameter dome is lined with glowing copper and supported by reinforced concrete beams. The floor is polished concrete. Natural light floods in through 180 vertical glass panels of differing sizes set between the dome and the rugged, roughly hewn rock walls. The dome appears to hover above the light which, depending on the angle of the rays, patterns the interior with colour.

The reds, mauves and greys used within the decor reflect the shades found in the granite itself. Native birch wood benches seat 750 people, the simple altar is a polished granite slab, the stark pulpit formed from reinforced concrete and the crucifix, candelabra, font and textiles are all the work of Finnish artists.

With an overhead gallery, fine organ, a split-level platform for a choir and an area reserved for an orchestra, this is a popular venue for weddings and classical music concerts.

The church is known for its superb acoustics, although that wasn't an attribute especially focussed on in the original plan. When Finnish conductor and violinist Paavo Berglund suggested to the acoustical engineer working on the project that, by leaving the rock exposed, it would vastly improve the sound quality within the church, the architects were happy to comply. The walls with their rough and virtually unworked surfaces have become one of the defining features of the popular Rock Church.

The award-winning Kamppi Chapel of Silence is a more recent example of Finnish architectural vision. Opened in 2012 in the busiest part of Helsinki's city centre, right outside a shopping mall, the chapel is an oasis of calm, a place for people to have a moment of silence, to stop, be still and unwind.

Its contemporary, vase-like design of curved wood with a gently shaped, uncluttered interior and diffused natural light creates an enveloping sense of welcome and warmth. Regular moments of prayer are held here but there are no official church services. Outside in an adjoining space, clergy and social workers are on hand to offer a listening ear.

– FRANCE –

CATHEDRAL OF NOTRE-DAME, STRASBOURG

Spectacular in every way, this vast cathedral full of exquisite detail resembles a Bible in stone. Its location is perfect, at the heart of the city, in a wide, cobblestoned square among Renaissance houses and half-timbered buildings, in the UNESCO-listed Old Town. It stands on an island formed by a division in the River Ill, the area around it so spacious the building can easily be seen in all its glory from every angle.

Strasbourg is situated on the border between France and Germany and has long been at the crossroads of two cultures. The history of the region has been turbulent and down the centuries both countries have claimed the city as a national emblem.

The cathedral is indisputably French High Gothic but the single, slender tower was built under the aegis of several German architects and bears a strong resemblance to those of Cologne's cathedral (page 127). Surmounted by a 144-metre (472-foot)-high spire, a pyramid of pinnacles delicate in its complexity, it is among the tallest in both France and Germany.

The foundations are Romanesque, from a basilica commissioned in 1015 but destroyed by fire in 1176. Construction on this cathedral began at the end of the 12th century and was completed three centuries later, in 1439.

Built in Vosges sandstone, in the changing light of the day its colour can range from cool grey-pink to a glowing ochre-red. Intricate, lace-like, carved stone details, flying buttresses and countless pinnacles, statues, angelic musicians and fantastical gargoyles, cover the exterior.

The tympanum above the central portal of the great west front is a wonder of scenes from the Old and New Testaments and the Passion of Christ, surrounded by layer upon layer of apostles, saints, martyrs, prophets, Biblical figures and winged angels. There are statues of the Virgin Mary and above them all, Christ sits in majesty and judgement, his throne attended by playful lions.

The arched portals to the left and right are decorated with graceful interpretations of virtues and vices, the parable of the wise and foolish virgins and scenes from the childhood of Christ. High above, the outline of the great rose window, 12.5 metres (41 feet) in diameter, tempts the visitor inside to view its brilliance.

The soaring Gothic nave, beautifully proportioned with seven bays and rising over three levels, has two side aisles. Towering windows in jewel colours flood the cathedral's interior with light.

Depicted within them are emperors of the Holy Roman Empire, the ancestors of Christ following the genealogy in St Luke's Gospel, episodes from the New Testament, heaven, hell, an army of popes and bishops and a procession of female saints led by the Virgin Mary.

Twice a year, when the sun is shining at the spring and autumn equinoxes, a shaft of green light seems to emerge from the shoe of Judas in a south window to focus on and illuminate the head of Christ on the pulpit. The 'green flash' lasts for about fifteen minutes.

Much of the glass dates from the 12th to the 14th centuries, but two stunning new windows were installed in St Catherine's Chapel in the autumn of the cathedral's 1,000th anniversary in 2015. At 7.8 metres (26 feet) high, innovative both in design and execution, they consist of 40 panes of digitally printed glass and reflect the artist Véronique Ellena's view of the diversity and beauty of the world.

On one side is a bright homage to nature, on the other, a powerful image of the face of Christ, the fingers of his right hand raised in blessing. Up close you can discern that within the face are smaller faces – it is a sepia photomontage. She photographed ordinary people visiting the cathedral and incorporated 150 images in the design.

At the heart of the nave, and richly carved in white sandstone, the hexagonal pulpit features some 50 small figures and flamboyant carving on the curving balustrade. Look for the small dog sleeping at its base. It's said that his clergyman master gave such long sermons that the poor dog would fall asleep – and lives on in stone as a reminder to subsequent preachers.

Head for the transept and marvel at its two major highlights, the unique Pillar of Angels and the fascinating astronomical clock. Dating from around 1230 and amazingly serving as the central pillar of the south transept, the slim, exquisitely carved Pillar of Angels features the four evangelists and trumpeting angels, all of whom seem to be stepping out from

Photo: Beijaflor

the stone. At the top, a serene Christ the Judge is attended by angels holding the instruments of his Passion.

Look up to the balcony beyond, where a small figure in the corner is keeping watch. He is a disbelieving builder who, convinced that the pillar could not support the vault, declared that he would just wait for the structure to collapse. He's had a long wait.

Built in the 1550s, the 18-metre (60-foot)-high astronomical clock, its mechanism said to be unique, puts on its display at 12.30 pm daily. A cherub rings a bell, another turns over an hourglass; the twelve Apostles process in adoration before Christ and, below them, figures representing the four ages of man march past Death. On the top, a golden cockerel crows and flaps its wings.

As well as giving the time, its dials include a perpetual calendar, an ecclesiastical calendar revealing the date of Easter, solar time, signs of the zodiac, phases of the moon and the position of several planets. Ancient deities in chariots indicate the days of the week.

The Romanesque choir stands above the nave and transept crossing, a cupola decorated with neo-Byzantine frescoes in its apse. Its elevation indicates its position above the crypt, the oldest part of the building and containing tombs of former bishops.

The warm and welcoming stained glass window of the Virgin and Child in the apse was a gift from the Council of Europe in 1956, a replacement for one destroyed during the Second World War. It features the flag of the European Union and shows the child Jesus holding a lily, emblem of the city of Strasbourg.

For panoramic views across the city's red rooftops, narrow streets and resplendent squares, past the European Parliament and encircling river, be prepared for a tough climb: the spiral staircase has 332 steps to the 66-metre (217-foot)-high viewing platform. On a suitably clear day, you can see as far as the Vosges' vineyards in France and the Black Forest in Germany.

VÉZELAY ABBEY, BURGUNDY

A masterpiece of Romanesque architecture and sculpture, in the Middle Ages the Basilique Sainte-Marie-Madeleine de Vézelay was a hugely important pilgrimage church believed to hold relics of St Mary Magdalene, the penitent and follower of Jesus Christ, to whom it is dedicated. It was (and still is) the starting point for a major route through France on the pilgrims' road to Santiago de Compostela in northern Spain.

A Benedictine monastery was built there in 860 and shortly afterwards a monk named Baudillon brought what were believed to be the bones of Mary Magdalene to Vézelay from Saint-Maximin-la-Sainte-Baume in Provence. Pilgrims soon followed and when in 1048 the Pope declared the relics to be authentic, the numbers increased rapidly.

Raiders and fires destroyed early buildings and the present church dates from the 12th century, much of it originally consecrated in 1104. In 1120 a disastrous fire not only caused serious damage to the building, it killed over 1,000 pilgrims.

The prior started work immediately on rebuilding the nave, completing it by 1140, but this, too, was destroyed by fire 25 years later. The soaring nave of translucent limestone that we admire today dates from its rebuilding.

A bigger entrance area, needed to accommodate so many pilgrims, resulted in the splendid narthex, completed in 1150; the vast, Early Gothic choir dates from 1185. Its design was way ahead of its time. Gothic architecture had only recently made an appearance in Paris and the great Gothic cathedrals had yet to be built.

As the number of pilgrims increased, so the community of monks expanded, reaching over 800 at one point, and Vézelay became a focus for some historically important events.

St Bernard of Clairvaux made his impassioned call for the ill-fated Second Crusade against the Saracens here in 1146 and twenty years later, St Thomas Becket, Archbishop of Canterbury then living in exile, excommunicated the courtiers of King Henry II and threatened the king with the same action. In 1190, King Richard I (the Lionheart) of England and the French king, Philip II, met and assembled their forces at Vézelay for the Third Crusade.

A more peaceful event happened in 1271 when Brother Pacifico, one of the companions of St Francis of Assisi, established the first French community of Friars Minor nearby.

In 1279, an announcement by Saint-Maximin-la-Sainte-Baume that Mary Magdalene's intact body had been 'discovered', shook Vézelay's foundations. As the Angevin King Charles II supported the spurious claim and, with the approval and encouragement of Pope Boniface VIII, built a magnificent basilica in honour of St Mary Magdalene there, the pilgrims moved on to Provence.

Vézelay went into decline, finally falling into severe disrepair. During the Wars of Religion in the late 16th century, Huguenot Protestants wrought their anger, burned the now-discredited relics and sacked the monastery. During the French Revolution the west façade was severely damaged and original sculptures destroyed.

Salvation came in the 19th century when the French architect Eugène Viollet-le-Duc was appointed to carry out major renovation and reconstruction (1840–61). The abbey church, which is only 9 metres (30 feet) shorter than Notre-Dame Cathedral in Paris, was elevated to basilica status in 1920 and designated a World Heritage Site by UNESCO in 1979.

The beleaguered west front may be underwhelming, but just step inside. The narthex – a huge enclosed forecourt separating the main entrance and the nave – has three remarkable doorways.

The tympanum above the central door is probably the finest Romanesque stone carving in France depicting Christ and the Apostles. They may have suffered some desecration since they were carved in the 1100s – many figures have featureless faces or missing limbs – but the overall effect is stunning.

The centrepiece is the risen Christ, with rays of light from his outstretched arms falling on the heads of the Apostles. He appears to be giving them their mission, to spread the Gospel to all nations and so we see, curving around him, narrative carvings with figures representing the 'heathen' peoples of the then-unknown world. In 29 medallions, zodiac signs tell of the months and the labours of the working year. People of the earth and their animals stride across the lintel below – note the elephant ears of the unbelievers.

To the left, the north-west door tympanum depicts the Road to Emmaus and Christ's Ascension; to the right above the south-west door it's the story of the Nativity, from the Annunciation to the visit of the Magi. Below, an angel seems to be flying out of the stone.

Photo: Harmonia Amanda

Step through the doors and you are into a catch-your-breath moment as the columns and arches of the nave and side aisles seem to soar away into the far distance. Natural light fills the Gothic choir and ambulatory like a beacon, drawing visitors forward to the altar.

The 62-metre (204-foot)-long nave has ten bays of powerful limestone columns in peaceful shades of coffee and cream. High above in the vault, arches are defined and patterned by stone stripes of alternating colours. Each of the 100 or so carved capitals, the majority of them 12th-century originals, has a story to tell.

Look for Moses and St Paul milling grain to make flour, a suitably tempting Eve plucking an apple from entwined branches, Noah, his wife and a basketry ark, Daniel in the lion's den and a rather spectacular David, slaying the giant Goliath. Binoculars come in handy here.

The basilica still has small relics of St Mary Magdalene, although not the ones they originally sheltered. These relics, a gift from Pope Martin IV to the Diocese of Sens in 1281, were presented to the abbey in the 1870s by the then Archbishop of Sens and are contained in a fine gold reliquary.

Today the building is in the care of the monks and nuns of the Fraternité Monastique de Jérusalem, who combine monastic life with their work in the town. The medieval village of Vézelay, strung out along the crest of a hill amid verdant countryside, grew up as a result of the abbey's pilgrimage status. Every year, many thousands of visitors still climb its long, steep main street on their way to the hilltop basilica.

NOTRE-DAME DE LA GARDE, MARSEILLES

At the top of La Garde, the highest natural point in the port city of Marseilles, this ornate 19th-century basilica dedicated to Our Lady is a treasure house of marble, murals and stunning mosaics. Locals often refer to their beloved church on the hill as La Bonne Mère (the Good Mother) who is guardian and protector of their city.

Full of eye-catching colour, the Neo-Byzantine upper church has dazzling golden domes and cupolas, inlaid marble, striped stone arches and exquisite mosaics inspired by the 5th- and 6th-century mosaics in Rome and Ravenna.

In complete contrast, the neo-Romanesque crypt is low and very simple, with statues of saints in side chapels and standing out against columns and arches. It was dug out of the solid rock and completed three years before the upper part of the basilica, with the first Mass celebrated there in 1861. A copy of the golden statue that crowns the basilica is used for the evening procession of the popular annual pilgrimage, which takes place on 15th August, the Feast of the Assumption.

Angels sounding trumpets top the square bell tower with its blind arcades and corners patterned with stripes of green and white stone. It is crowned with the gilded statue of Our Lady who holds out her infant son, his arms raised in blessing, above her flowing robes.

In 1214, a priest built a small chapel dedicated to the Virgin Mary on the rocky top of a 161-metre (528-foot)-high limestone hill, known as La Garde, above the then small town of Marseilles. When the young King Francois I visited 300 years later, he was concerned to see how poor the town's defences were.

After the Holy Roman Emperor King Charles V attempted to besiege Marseilles in 1524, Francois had two fortresses built: one on the island of If, offshore in the bay (later to be made famous by Alexandre Dumas in *The Count of Monte Cristo*) and the other on top of the Garde Hill. Encompassing the chapel, the castle fortress was known as Fort Notre-Dame de la Garde.

Surprisingly, the chapel remained open to the public, who crossed a drawbridge to visit it, and it became popular with sailors who often came back with votive offerings in thanks for their safe return and prayers heard. Today you still cross a drawbridge at the top of the main stairs to enter the crypt and votive offerings are seen everywhere in the basilica.

During the French Revolution, members of the Bourbon family were imprisoned in the fortress for six months and by the end of 1793 the Catholic Church had been supressed and the chapel's assets seized.

The town had grown considerably when services began again in 1807 and the chapel was too small to accommodate all the worshippers. The fortress was state property but a small extension was agreed. Then in 1852 permission was given to replace the chapel with a bigger church.

The architect chosen for the task was a 23-year-old Protestant, Jacques Henri Espérandieu. The style was to be neo-Romanesque; its later decoration with Byzantine-inspired mosaics means it is usually referred to as Romano-Byzantine.

Twenty-three shiploads of marble and porphyry were brought from Italy for the building with 12 million tesserae used to create the mosaics.

The first stone was laid in 1853 but money was tight and eight years on just the crypt had been excavated with little to show of the basilica itself. The sanctuary was consecrated in 1864, the bell tower completed two years later and the monumental statue of Our Lady, covered in gold leaf, was hauled into place in 1870.

The statue is 11 metres (36 feet) tall, weighs almost 10 tonnes and can be seen from across town and for miles out to sea, acting as a beacon to the sailors and fishermen of this port city. Work continued on the interior for a further twenty years and concluded with the positioning of the heavy bronze doors in 1897.

The fort was demilitarised in 1934 after an agreement that the army would give the top of Garde Hill to the diocese in exchange for a property in the centre of Marseilles. However, the papers weren't signed, nor the exchange made official until 1941. A year after the French army left La Garde, the Germans invaded south-eastern France and their soldiers occupied the fortress.

The basilica came under heavy fire during its liberation in 1944 and repairing the tesserae of mosaics lost during bombing raids was among the restoration works carried out at the turn of the new millennium. New buildings have been added over the years and beneath the great walls, Le Musée d'Art sacré unravels some history.

Two marble statues flank the porch at the entrance to the upper church. The prophet Isaiah holds a scroll engraved with his prophecy of the birth of Jesus; the Apostle John's scroll bears words from the Book of the Apocalypse referring to the Virgin Mary.

Inside, the basilica resounds to a tapestry of colours, with soaring red and white striped marble columns and arches outlining glittering glass mosaics.

Above the nave, three cupolas in glowing gold feature fields of flowers with doves in flight around a central floret.

Photo: Robert Valette

Events from the Old Testament are depicted in medallions in the corners where the cupola meets the pillars.

In the transept crossing, four angels in a field of gold support a wreath of roses around the jewel-studded monogram that crowns the inside of the dome. Decorative bands of stylised flowers pattern walls and ceilings; geometric designs cover the floor.

A silver statue of the Virgin and Child weighing 80 kilograms (176 lb) stands at the white marble main altar. A replacement for the statue melted down by French Revolutionaries, it was crowned in June 1931 during solemn festivities that lasted four days, was attended by 49 bishops and attracted vast crowds to Marseilles.

Behind the altar, the brilliantly coloured apse features a sailing ship in its central medallion. It is set among trails of greenery inhabited by peacocks and exotic birds in a golden, flower-filled world.

Notre-Dame de la Garde is noted for its huge number of votive offerings, from beautifully crafted ships hanging from on high to paintings, planes and portraits, letters, flags, plaques and banners, left by grateful petitioners in thanks for divine assistance.

If the interior is spectacular, so is the view from the terraces where a panorama unfolds across the city, the mountains, the islands and far out into the bay.

– GERMANY –

COLOGNE CATHEDRAL, COLOGNE

Considered the greatest Gothic cathedral in Germany and dedicated to St Peter and the Virgin Mary, Cologne's mighty cathedral (Kölner Dom) was built to be a suitably grand resting place for the relics of the Magi (the Three Wise Men of the Nativity story), which had been acquired by Cologne in 1164.

Building commenced in 1248 – its completion over 600 years later in 1880 was a nationally celebrated event. The Dom's twin towers, soaring to a height of over 157 metres (515 feet), are a symbol of the city.

Although the great west front – the world's largest church façade – was only built in the 19th century, its design is faithful to the original medieval plans and there's a marvellous sense of High Gothic unity throughout the building. In granting Cologne's cathedral World Heritage status in 1996, UNESCO stated: 'No other cathedral is so perfectly conceived, so uniformly and uncompromisingly executed in all its parts.'

Its sheer size and grandeur is overwhelming. The slim nave, flanked by two aisles on each side, rises heavenwards to the 43-metre (141-foot)-high vaulted ceiling. Magnificent stained glass windows bathe the warm stone interior with light. Massive statues of saints and biblical figures hang on the nave's arcade of elegant clustered pillars and lead the eye to the chancel ahead.

The crossing, originally intended as the setting for

Photo: Tobi 87

the Shrine of the Magi, is the cathedral's liturgical heart and is furnished with a 20th-century archbishop's throne (cathedra) in carved cherry wood, altar, bronze communion rails and lectern. The oak pulpit with its expressive sculptures, however, has been used in the cathedral since the 15th century.

In the Choir, the 14th-century oak choir stalls have carvings and misericords on the 104 seats. Behind the stalls, choir screens (1332–40) painted in glowing colours tell the stories of saints and biblical figures, emperors, kings and archbishops. On the pillars, smiling angels playing musical instruments stand above the tall figures of Christ, the Virgin Mary and the twelve Apostles. In the clerestory, the fifteen colourful 'royal windows' are the largest surviving cycle of early 14th-century glass in Europe.

The massive black marble high altar was consecrated in 1322. Behind it, the Shrine of the Magi is the greatest of all the cathedral's treasures and the largest reliquary in the Western world. Covered in gilded silver, studded with jewels, surrounded with relief figures and bearing three crowned skulls, it was created between 1190 and 1220.

One of the most beautiful examples of the medieval goldsmiths' art, its shape is that of three shrines, two below and one above. The images depicted include scenes from the history of salvation to the Last Judgement, from Old Testament prophets and the Adoration of the Magi through the life, death and Resurrection of Christ. Surrounding the figures are delicate filigree panels set with precious stones as well as cameos, columns and arches trimmed with blue and white enamels.

Seven semi-circular chapels, containing tombs and epitaphs of Cologne's archbishops and some very fine medieval paintings and sculptures, surround the chancel.

Side chapels in aisles, too, contain some wonderful works of art.

In the Chapel of the Cross, off the north aisle, the monumental Gero Crucifix is a powerful, larger than life-sized image, carved from oak in 970. Made in Cologne and named for its archbishop donor, it became the model for countless medieval crucifixes.

Across in the south aisle, the Lady Chapel contains the Altar of the City Patrons, an exquisitely detailed triptych painted by Stefan Lochner, an artist of the Cologne School, in around 1440. When closed (during Advent and Lent) it shows the Annunciation; when opened it reveals the Adoration of the Magi flanked by patron saints of Cologne St Ursula and St Gereon, each attended by their martyred companions.

Nearby, the 13th-century Milan Madonna, crowned in gold with a halo of stars, is said to have miraculous powers. High Gothic and carved in wood, the flowing folds of her gown, painted in shades of blue, gold and crimson, are remarkably realistic. The silk dress of the 17th-century Baroque Jewelled Madonna, found in the north transept, is always pinned with precious votive offerings in thanksgiving for prayers heard.

Amid the feast of medieval art and sculpture, the don't-miss highlights include the Altarpiece of St Clare in the north aisle, which at 6 metres (20 feet) wide is the largest 14th-century altar in the cathedral and has a built-in tabernacle. In the south transept seek out the large Altarpiece of St Agilolphus. Made in Antwerp around 1520, its central section is filled with hundreds of carved and painted figures depicting scenes from the life and Passion of Christ.

The oldest glass in the cathedral is in the Chapel of the Three Kings, dating from 1280, and is the earliest preserved 'Bible window' in Germany. Several windows in the choir chapels, a large cycle of kings in the clerestory and several in the north nave aisle date from the early days of building in the 13th and 14th centuries. Many of the brilliantly coloured windows in the north aisle date from the 16th century, those in the south aisle from the 19th century.

A monumental new window by Cologne artist Gerhard Richter was installed in 2007. It features over 11,000 squares made of mouth blown glass in 72 different colours. The Life of Christ windows on the ground floor of the towers have recently been reconstructed from 19th-century designs, the originals having been almost totally destroyed in the Second World War. When Allied bombing flattened and turned the city surrounding it to rubble, the cathedral was left standing but severely damaged. While essential repair work was finished in 1956, restoration continues to this day.

Built between 1997 and 2000, partly using underground medieval space and partly as a new build on the cathedral's north side, Cologne Cathedral's attractive Treasury is the biggest and probably the richest in Germany. Among the chalices and monstrances, reliquaries, vestments and illuminated manuscripts are some early examples of Christian art that are over 1,000 years old.

The climb to the 100-metre (328-foot)-high viewing platform in the south tower entails 533 steps. Along the way you pass the bell chamber where the St Peter's bell, weighing in at 24 tonnes, is the largest free-swinging church bell in the world.

The cathedral is huge and very splendid. It is also very busy. Every year it welcomes 6 million visitors through its doors.

AACHEN CATHEDRAL, AACHEN

Around the year 800, the emperor Charlemagne built his Church of St Mary to be an image of the Heavenly Jerusalem. Packed with symbolism, it brought together architecture from the Eastern and Western parts of the Holy Roman Empire and attracted pilgrims from all over the known world. Between 936 and 1531 it was the setting for the coronation of 30 German kings and twelve queens.

Aachen's cathedral is a surprising and visually striking building. Its architecture spans centuries and its shimmering mosaics, glimmering gold and towering stained glass windows stay long in the memory. In 1978, the cathedral was on the very first list of twelve natural and cultural wonders to be designated a World Heritage Site by UNESCO, along with the rock churches of Lalibela in Ethiopia (page 232).

Crowned Roman Emperor by Pope Leo III in 800, Charlemagne had ambitious plans to create a new Rome, with Aachen at the centre of his empire (which covered most of Western Europe) and his church its religious heart. The Palatine chapel in his extensive palace complex at Aachen, which had been built on the site of Roman baths, forms the core of today's cathedral.

Modelled on Byzantine churches of the time, especially the Basilica of San Vitale in Ravenna, the high-domed octagonal centre was surrounded by a sixteen-sided outer wall. This supported a high gallery above, creating a church on two levels, the upper storey being referred to as the Hochmünster (high church). This is where you'll find the high altar, imperial throne and the golden sarcophagus containing the bones of Charlemagne, who died in 814.

Photo: Carschten

Charlemagne sourced the finest building materials from his empire, raiding Rome and Ravenna and bringing ancient columns from Cologne for the upper gallery. Master masons, artists and craftsmen, too, came from far and wide.

The great bronze doors from his church stand at the cathedral's main west front entrance. Each one weighs 2.5 tonnes and was cast in one piece at the start of the 9th century. The decoration bears references to doors found in ancient Rome. Likewise the Carolingian bronze rails in the upper church were modelled on similar Roman designs.

Entering through the atrium you find a bronze pine cone, its drilled tips indicating that it once topped the fountain that originally stood here. It dates from around 1000 and at its base are personifications of the 'rivers of paradise', the Tigris and Euphrates in Mesopotamia.

The fountain mirrors that in Old St Peter's, a symbol of the spiritual power of Rome. The bronze she-wolf nearby, probably from the 3rd century BC, corresponds with the Capitoline Wolf from the legendary founding of Rome and symbolised worldly power in Aachen, the new Rome. After a coronation, the ruler would swear an oath on the pine cone to guarantee the welfare of the people and on the she-wolf to ensure their protection.

Stepping into the octagon (Charlemagne's church) is an assault on the senses, with colour upon colour, pattern upon pattern, and an overarching glow of gold. Striped arches connect sturdy pillars in two levels of arcades rising up to a heavenly cupola. Light enters through arched windows in the octagonal drum between the upper storey and the cupola. Walls are lined with marble panels in alternating colours and mosaics glitter on vaulted ceilings.

The original mosaics in the cupola are long gone but they were recreated in the 19th century by a Venetian workshop.

Against a warm gold background and a field of stars, Christ is shown as the triumphant lord of the world, surrounded by the symbols of the four evangelists and the 24 elders from the Apocalypse of St John, all offering their crowns up to him. Finally the dome has an intricate pattern of mosaics with a *trompe l'oeil* effect.

Hanging from the dome and dominating the octagon, the great Barbarossa chandelier, 4.2 metres (14 feet) in diameter, was donated to the cathedral by Emperor Frederick I Barbarossa in the 12th century. Made of iron and gilded copper, it is composed of eight curved segments, studded with sixteen golden towers and bearing 48 candles. An inscription reveals that it was designed as an image of the heavenly Jerusalem, descending from the celestial skies. Engravings depict the Beatitudes from the Sermon on the Mount and scenes from the life of Christ.

On the upper ambulatory, six marble steps lead up to the imperial throne. Made from four slabs of white marble, believed to have come from holy sites in Jerusalem, assembled with bronze clamps and set between columns on four pillars, it is surprisingly unadorned and appealing in its simplicity.

It faces the high altar, on the opposite side of the octagon, which bears a spectacular gold frontal, the Pala D'Oro (Golden Table), dating from around 1020. Christ the Redeemer is enthroned with the Virgin Mary and Archangel Michael in a central mandala. Grouped around it are ten relief panels with scenes from the Passion of Christ.

The bejewelled and gilded pulpit, trefoil-shaped and made from copper in the 11th century, was the gift of Emperor Henry II. The Shrine of the Virgin Mary, spectacularly gold and wonderfully decorated, houses the cathedral's main relics.

Behind them and set apart, the gold Shrine of Charlemagne outshines them all. In the shape of a church, it is 2 metres (6.5 feet) long, dates from 1215 and is heavily decorated with reliefs, filigree, enamels and engravings. Figures represent kings and emperors, angels, saints, and the Madonna and Child. On the front gable end, the enthroned Charlemagne takes centre stage between Pope Leo III, who consecrated the Palatine chapel, and the Archbishop of Rheims who supported the emperor's canonisation.

A large, double-side wood sculpture of the Virgin Mary, attended by winged cherubs and set in a sunburst corona, hangs from the vault above.

This whole high altar area is backed by thirteen brilliantly coloured windows, soaring to a height of 26 metres (85 feet), a 15th-century Early Gothic addition modelled on the Sainte-Chapelle in Paris. The glass is modern (post-Second World War) and depicts the story of salvation, with ornamental panels resembling luminous curtains.

Already a pilgrimage church, when Charlemagne was canonised on Christmas Day in 1165, the number of pilgrims grew rapidly and extensions to the church became necessary. Five chapels, added in the 14th, 15th and 18th centuries in different sizes, architectural styles and decor, surround the octagon and together with other additions result in the larger building that is Aachen Cathedral.

Relics were an important part of any church in the Middle Ages and Aachen's were top notch: the cloak of the Blessed Virgin, the swaddling clothes of the baby Jesus, the loin cloth worn by Christ on the cross and the cloth that bore the head of St John the Baptist after his martyrdom.

Once every seven years since 1394, the relics are removed from the ornate gold Shrine of the Virgin Mary (where they were placed in the 13th century) and shown to public view. In June 2014, over 100,000 people joined the Aachen Pilgrimage to see and venerate them. They will be shown again in 2021.

In a feast of gold, jewels and glories of the goldsmiths' art, precious objects from the cathedral's history, many of them gifts from royalty, are kept in the well-designed Treasury in the cloister. Considered among the finest in Germany, the collection includes artefacts from late antiquity and medieval times, most famously a gold and silver reliquary bust of Charlemagne and the bejewelled Cross of Lothair, dating from around the year 1000.

MARIENKIRCHE, LÜBECK

The distinctive, green-roofed twin spires of St Mary's Church soar elegantly skywards above Lübeck's picture book Old Town. Built between 1250 and 1350, in a distinctive style that would become known as northern Brick Gothic (Backsteingotik), the new church expressed the importance, wealth, power and individuality of the city at the heart of the mighty Hanseatic League.

The natural stone on which the emerging Gothic architecture of France and England depended was in short supply in this part of the world. The use of locally fired and glazed bricks to build St Mary's was a bold adaptation of the towering Gothic style and influenced the design and construction of around 70 churches across the entire Baltic region.

The Marienkirche is one of the largest churches in Germany. Four million bricks were used in its building; at

Photo: W. Balach

over 38 metres (126 feet) its nave is the highest brick vault in the world, and until Cologne Cathedral (page 127) was completed, those 125-metre (409-foot)-high towers with their verdigris-coated spires were the world's tallest twin church towers.

Inside, all is space and light. The nave and its two side aisles are of equal length, their pale and slender ribbed piers and vaults painted in warm earth colours and gentle patterns.

Chapels radiate off the ambulatory and adjoin the aisles, some serving as sepulchral chapels and bearing the names of the families of the city councillors that endowed them. The Chapel of Indulgences (renamed Briefkapelle during the Reformation when official letter writers moved in) built around 1310, is one of the earliest examples of star vaulting in Europe. Pure High Gothic, it is used for church services in the coldest winter months.

Lübeck's wealthy merchants and city councillors built the Marienkirche after a major dispute with the city's bishopric. They were determined that their church, which they sited near the City Hall and market, would be bigger, taller and more modern (hence Gothic) than the Romanesque cathedral down the road. Not only was translating the Gothic style into brick a major innovation, a brave act that would be copied elsewhere down the centuries, in the 14th century it was the largest church in Christendom.

At this time, Lübeck was known as a centre of craftsmanship. In the 14th and 15th centuries its artists and carvers supplied altars to monasteries and cathedrals in Scandinavia and Hanseatic cities along the coast. The Lübeck master Bernt Notke, famed for his massive 'Dance of Death' mural painted during the plague years and his Triumphal Cross that still dominates Lübeck's cathedral, received commissions from wealthy clients across the Baltic region.

Mercantile wealth found its expression in architecture and the Hanseatic merchants filled their churches with art treasures. The Marienkirche was particularly well endowed. All that changed on the night of Palm Sunday, 28–29 March 1942, when RAF bombing raids (possibly in retaliation for the destruction of Coventry, page 58) devastated the medieval city.

Consumed by fire, bells rang out their last peal from the south tower before crashing down, the twisted pieces of two of them embedded in the floor. There they remain, where they fell, in the moving Chapel of Memory, a reminder of the futility of war. A Coventry Cross of Nails (page 58) sits in a niche nearby.

Restoration of the ruined church began in 1947. One treasure that did survive the bombing is the magnificent double-winged Antwerp Altar of St Mary, created in 1518. Showing scenes of the Virgin's life and death, depicted in painting and gilded carving, it stands triumphantly in the apse of Lady Chapel (also known as the Singers' Chapel, for it once had its own choir).

Music has always played an important role – the Marienkirche is known to have had an organ back in the 14th century. The composer Dieterich Buxtehude was organist here from 1668 until his death in 1707 and introduced the first evening concerts, a tradition that continues to this day. Georg Friedrich Handel visited in 1703 and in 1705, the young Johann Sebastian Bach walked near on 400 kilometres (250 miles) to hear Buxtehude play, staying three months in his company.

In 1968 a replacement main organ was installed. Built by the Lübeck organ builders Kemper & Son, it had the largest mechanical action in the world. Paul Behrens, a Lübeck clockmaker, decided to recreate the 16th-century astronomical clock lost in the earlier fire, and from 1960 spent seven years working on it, making all the parts himself. The face is a simplified version of the original but the workings are remarkable. It shows the day and month, the planetary positions of the sun and moon, the astronomical signs of the zodiac and a liturgical calendar with the dates of Easter. The clock chimes at noon when a procession of eight figures representing the Christian peoples of the world passes a figure of Christ, which offers a hand of blessing.

Plaster dislodged by the heat of the conflagration revealed original Gothic decorative features that had been painted over during the Reformation. Using photographic documentation made during the war, in 1948 artists were employed to recreate the frescoes. Unfortunately there were no references for the chancel and local artist Lothar Malskat invented them in the style of the 14th century. He admitted what he'd done, got a prison sentence for forgery, and the offending fakes were removed.

Most of the replacement windows were leaded in simple diamond panes with coats of arms of the donors, but the lyrics of one of Buxtehude's Lübeck cantatas were included in the Singer's Chapel. Two 1950s stained glass windows depict characters from the lost medieval frieze 'Dance of Death' with the bottom panes showing Lübeck in flames.

A cheeky little devil, sculpted in bronze in 1999, sits on a block of granite outside the church. Legend tells that the devil, believing that the building was to be a tavern, helped the church's construction to grow quickly. When he realised he'd been misled, he was all for throwing that great stone and smashing the work, but was promised that a building would rise to keep him happy – and opposite the church is the Ratskeller, the wine cellar of the Town Hall.

Romanesque sculptures and other treasures from St Mary's can be found in Lübeck's excellent St Annen Museum. The walls and cloisters of this 16th-century former convent are a perfect backdrop for its fine collection of medieval ecclesiastical art. Upstairs, a maze of furnished rooms reveals the splendour of Hanseatic lifestyles.

– HUNGARY –

MÁTYÁS-TEMPLOM, BUDAPEST

Crowning the Buda Hills and officially named the Buda Castle Church of Our Lady, but much better known as the Matthias Church, the outline of the templom's tower, spire and distinctive tiled roof forms a focal landmark high above the fast-flowing Danube River that separates the two halves of the city of Budapest.

The turrets, spires and pinnacles of this church of delightful surprises echo the country's turbulent history. Founded in the 13th century, a coronation church for Hungarian kings, it was used as a mosque by the Ottoman Turks for over 150 years. Then, in the 19th century, a radical rebuilding exercise took out anything that wasn't medieval and remodelled the church in neo-Gothic style. In bright orange, turquoise and earthy ochre tones, Zsolnay glazed tiles pattern the roof and even clad spires in lively diamond and zigzag designs.

Founded by King Bela IV, who moved his royal residence from Esztergom on the Danube bend to the Buda hills once the invading Mongols had left in 1242, the church was expanded in Gothic style by King Matthias Corvinus the Fair in the 15th century. No saint but a mythical hero of many Hungarian legends, this is the Matthias after whom the church gets its popular name.

By the time the Turks were routed after the siege of Buda in 1686, not a lot had survived the Ottoman rule and the rebuilt Matthias church took on a Baroque persona. It was restored back to the Gothic style in the late 19th century. The last two Hungarian Habsburg kings were crowned here: Franz Joseph in 1867, for whom Franz Liszt wrote and performed his *Coronation Mass*, and Charles IV in 1916.

Inside, a sense of mystery pervades, with walls covered in paintings by two outstanding 19th-century Hungarian painters, Károly Lotz and Bertalan Székely, in colours inspired by the Orient. Every inch of every surface is painted, mainly with geometric and floral motifs. Whirls of entwined gold outline the gentle sky blue in the nave ceiling vaults. The superb stained glass windows with their strong figures, intricate rosettes and intensely coloured roundels also bear the signatures of Lotz and Székely.

After the initial impact of pattern and colour as you enter the church through two huge oak doors, a closer look reveals that the slim columns and arches have their own individual designs and yet coalesce into a unified whole.

Here, neo-Gothic and neo-Renaissance motifs meet elements of Art Nouveau and the romanticism of the Pre-Raphaelites and the Arts and Crafts movement as epitomised by William Morris. Stylised flowers meet playful geometrics and Hungarian folk art as pattern stacks up on pattern and colours contrast yet never clash.

There are religious subjects – look for the glimmering gold evangelists over the crossing – and scenes from

Photo: Nikolai Karaneschev

Hungary's history with figures that could have stepped from an illustrated book of fairy tales. Gold catches the light to lift any heaviness on the neo-Gothic triptych altarpiece; it outlines angel frescoes and frames deep-set windows.

Beneath the south tower, a statue of the Virgin Mary and the Christ child from 1515 is the treasure to be found in the Loreto Chapel. It survived the Turks' use of the church as a mosque because locals had secretly plastered over the niche in which it stood.

In these surroundings, the regular classical concerts held here in the summer are special occasions. The entrance ticket to the church includes entry into the Ecclesiastical Gallery and it's a trail well worth following.

Extensively damaged and desecrated during the Soviet and German occupations towards the end of the Second World War, the church was restored by the Hungarian government, but with poor quality materials, in the ensuing communist era. Add to this pollution, and the tramp of tourist feet as the city attracted ever more foreign visitors, by the time the new millennium approached the Matthias Church wasn't at its best.

Some serious restoration, carried out between 2006 and 2013, including 150,000 new roof tiles reproduced by the Zsolnay factory in Pécs, the installation of new flooring and the careful conservation of the stained glass, murals and paintings, has left it glowing with colour inside and out.

Outside in the square, a powerful equestrian statue of St Stephen, the first king of Hungary who founded the original church on this site in 1015, stands above the white marble extravaganza that is the Fishermen's Bastion. Its arches frame the renowned view across the Danube to the Pest side of the city, where the domed St Stephen's Basilica is also a church with impact, but in a very different style.

– ICELAND –

HALLGRÍMSKIRKJA, REYKJAVÍK

Inspired by Iceland's dramatic landscapes and named for the country's favourite pastor and poet, Hallgrímur Pétursson, this is Iceland's largest church (capacity 1,200 worshippers) and an unforgettable Reykjavík landmark. Like basalt cliffs it appears to rise organically from its hilltop site, the white concrete wings starting low then sweeping upwards, in perfect symmetry, to flank the central 73-metre (244-foot)-high tower that's visible for miles across the city.

The then State Architect Guðjón Samúelsson submitted his design for the church in 1937. He was inspired by natural shapes and forms and drew on Icelandic traditions and materials, seeking a distinctive style of architecture that would be in harmony with the landscape. In his vision for Hallgrím's church, mountains and glaciers soar up through hexagonal columns of basalt formed by cooling lava.

Construction began in 1945; three years later the crypt was consecrated and services were held there until the completion of the tower section in 1974. The whole church was finally consecrated in 1986, on the 312th anniversary of the death of Hallgrímur Pétursson.

The Reverend Hallgrímur (1614–1674) is best known for his *Hymns of Passion*. The 50 hymns, one for each working day of the seven weeks of Lent, reflect on Christ's Passion and death. In time-honoured tradition, they are still sung in services throughout Lent, when verses from them are read out daily on Icelandic national radio. There are many

Image: rheins

references to him and his work within the church and he is depicted, singing lustily, in the slim stained glass window above the entrance to the church.

Beneath the window, big bronze doors bid a welcome with the words 'Come to Me' alongside a quatrefoil panel on a red mosaic background. On this are portrayed bronze images of Christ on the right and man on the left, braided together with a crown of thorns that ends in the door handle. Here the hand of God and man are united. Inside, the door handle forms a cross, surrounded by symbols of the Gospel and the four archangels.

Unadorned and luminous, the interior rises to great heights from slim columns and sinuous lines that curve to meet in gently pointed arches. The pale wood of the pews and pulpit offers a little colour to interrupt the church's austere whiteness.

Glass panels on the pulpit reproduce a page from Hallgrímur's manuscript of *Hymns of the Passion*, traditional symbols of the Holy Trinity and Christ's monogram, the Greek letters chi-rho, flanked by the letters alpha and omega. A bowl of Czech lead crystal like shimmering ice sits above a base of Icelandic basalt to form the clean lines of the baptismal font.

To many visitors, the architectural design of hexagonal concrete columns increasing in height is reminiscent of organ pipes. Inside the church, the impressive concert organ that attracts professional organists from around the world to play and make recordings is 15 metres (50 feet) tall, weighs 25 tonnes and has 5,275 pipes, the largest being 10 metres (33 feet) long.

Constructed by German organ builders, it has the hallmarks of the simple lines and equilibrium that defines so much of Icelandic design. Regular organ concerts here are popular events and an annual international organ festival is held over the summer months.

The church is a striking presence on the Reykjavík skyline and its bell tower is one of the city's most visited tourist attractions. An elevator speeds to the viewing platform for panoramic views across town and out to the mountains and ocean beyond.

In the grounds outside, a commanding statue by Alexander Stirling Calder sees Norse explorer Leif Eriksson striding out in conquering mode. It pre-dates the church, being a gift from the United States on the 1,000th anniversary of the establishment of Iceland's parliament, held at Thingvellir in 930. A plaque declares that Eriksson was the first European to set foot in America, in the year 1000.

Surely one of the world's most dramatic houses of worship, it echoes the otherworldly atmosphere of the landscape that surrounds it. Its detractors find it too austere, Brutalist even, (though the architect had submitted his plan long before that movement started in the 1950s), but it has captured the hearts of those who view it as Expressionist architecture at its most appealing, and happily lose themselves in its elegant simplicity.

– ITALY –

THE PANTHEON, ROME

Completed around the year 125 under the rule of the Emperor Hadrian, in 609 this 'temple to all the gods' was

the first pagan temple in Rome to be transformed into a Christian church.

Somehow it survived the sieges and raids that shattered other Roman monuments, and although it has been battered and bruised down the centuries, having been stripped of its bronze surfaces and the gold on its great doors, it is undoubtedly the best preserved of the city's buildings of true antiquity.

Officially named the Basilica di Santa Maria ad Martyres, but known to all as the Pantheon, it is an architectural marvel. The 43.3-metre (142-foot)-diameter dome is still the single largest unreinforced concrete dome in the world. The proportions are perfect: the distance from the floor to the top of the dome is exactly equal to its diameter. A perfect sphere inscribed within a cylinder.

Michelangelo studied the Pantheon – which he described as looking more like the work of angels than men – before he began work on the dome of St Peter's Basilica in the Vatican and Brunelleschi gathered inspiration here for the dome of the Duomo in Florence. It has influenced buildings around the Western world, from the Panthéon in Paris to the State Library of Victoria in Melbourne, Australia and Thomas Jefferson's Rotunda at the University of Virginia in Charlottesville, USA.

The rotunda is faced by a front colonnade of eight massive Corinthian pillars, backed by two more rows of four columns each, quarried and transported from Egypt. They support the pediment that bears an inscription indicating that the Roman consul Marcus Agrippa was the builder – a gesture that credits the creator of the first Pantheon (which subsequently burned down) in 27 AD.

Entrance to the rotunda is via mighty, double bronze doors, each weighing 20 tonnes, and inside there's an immediate impression of sheer, expansive space.

The curvature of the dome draws the visitor's eye upwards. Encircling rows of concrete coffers reduce in size as they rise to the dome's centre, where a round opening, the oculus, is open to the elements and is the building's only source of natural light. Sun shines a disc of illumination, tracing a path over the roof, walls and floor, its size and span varying according to its position in the heavens. The oculus is 8.8 metres (29 feet) in diameter and any rain that falls through it drains away via well-concealed holes in the gently sloping floor.

That floor is the ancient Roman original, its design a series of geometric patterns in grey granite, red porphyry and yellow and purple marble.

Around the 6-metre (20-foot)-thick, marble-clad wall of the rotunda are seven alcoves, alternately semi-circular and rectangular, each flanked with two columns of either purple or yellow marble, finished with a pediment and furnished with wall niches.

The main altar of the church, opposite the entrance, has towering Corinthian columns in pink-red marble and the apse is filled with a golden mosaic, patterned with crosses decorated in blue and gold. Marble hangs like a sheltering curtain behind the altar table, where seven large candlesticks draw the eye up to an original 7th-century Byzantine icon of the Madonna and Child, framed in gold.

Monumental tombs are set into the walls, including those of the Renaissance artist Raphael and his long-suffering fiancée Maria Bibbiena. That of King Vittorio Emanuele II, the first king of a unified Italy, looks powerful in black while his successor, King Umberto I has a less ostentatious maroon-coloured pedestal.

On the days of the equinoxes in March and September the midday sun shines through the Pantheon's oculus at the perfect angle to pass through a grille above the doorway and light up the front courtyard – the only time it sees sunlight if the main doors are closed. Another architectural feat and one of many Pantheon mysteries still to be solved.

BASILICA OF SAN CLEMENTE, ROME

One of the most beautiful and fascinating of Rome's churches has a multitude of stories to tell. At street level it is a 12th-century basilica, but it sits atop a 4th-century church that in turn stands over a 2nd-century pagan temple and a 1st-century Roman house with a secret Christian chapel – and that replaced a villa and industrial building destroyed in the great fire of 64 AD. As an embodiment of Rome's layered history, a visit here is a journey deep into the Eternal City's past.

Dedicated to Pope St Clement, who died in 99 AD and was one of the earliest successors to St Peter as Bishop of Rome, the basilica was completed and consecrated around 1118–19. It is a gem.

Above the high altar and filled with early Christian symbolism, the Byzantine-style apse mosaic, titled the 'Triumph of the Cross' and probably dating from the 1130s, is the basilica's crowning jewel.

Against a light-catching gold background, its focal point is Christ on the Cross, portrayed as the Tree of Life. The Virgin Mary and John the Evangelist turn towards it in mourning and twelve white doves adorn the cross, symbolising the Apostles.

Sprouting vines whirl and twirl from a thriving acanthus bush at the base of the cross and nourish an abundance of life – exotic birds, stags, fruit-filled baskets, flowers, vases, oil lamps, a woman feeding chickens, a shepherd with his sheep and the Latin church fathers, Saints Gregory, Jerome, Augustine and Ambrose, dressed as monks and holding books.

Christ is thus presented as the life-giving source of all things in nature and culture. The vine motif is echoed in the nave's mosaic floor, seemingly extending the offer of paradise to all who enter the church.

The half dome of the apse is set within a triumphal arch that tells the story of salvation history. To the right of the arch, there's the city of Jerusalem, above it the prophet Jeremiah, with Saints Peter and Clement sitting enthroned at the top. To the left, Bethlehem is at the base, with the prophet Isaiah and then Saints Paul and Lawrence above it.

At the bottom of the apse, on a frieze of contrasting deep blue, six white sheep shown in profile are emerging from each of the biblical cities, on an orderly march to greet the central figure, the golden-haloed Lamb of God who looks out, face on, to the church. At the top, the Hand of God reaches down from the canopy of the jewelled heavens.

With a central nave and two side aisles divided by marble and granite columns, the basilica, or upper church, contains elements from several different centuries. In a strange mix-and-match effect, Baroque paintings and an 18th-century ornately painted and gilded ceiling watch over 4th-century marble choir screens (rescued from the lower church) decorated with the early Christian symbols of doves, vines and fish, as well as the wonderful Early Renaissance frescoes found in the Chapel of St Catherine of Alexandria, also known as the Castiglioni Chapel after its founder, Cardinal Branda da Castiglioni.

They were painted around 1428 by the Florentine artist Masolino da Panicale, and display the realism and perspective that were beginning to find favour in the artistic

world at this time. An exquisite Annunciation hovers above the arched entrance to the chapel where the walls show eight scenes from the life of St Catherine on the left hand wall and four episodes from the life of St Ambrose on the right. A multi-figured Crucifixion fills the end wall and the four Evangelists are paired with Church fathers, seated on clouds, on the vaulted ceiling.

Now descend the stairs to the 4th-century church. On a similar floor plan, this was in use until 1084 when, it is believed, during a siege by the Norman prince, Robert Guiscard, it was damaged beyond repair. Fragments of vibrant frescoes and mosaics survive and make up one of the largest collections of early medieval wall paintings in Rome. The last fresco on the left has an earthy quote: 'Go on, you sons of harlots, pull' – an early example of written vernacular Italian.

The air grows cooler and more humid, and the lighting ever more minimal, as you descend the stairs to the Mithraeum, a shrine to the god Mithras, where the altar block shows the god slaying a bull. The cult of Mithras originated in Persia and was the most venerated in the Roman Empire at the time. Believed to have been born in a cave, he was worshipped by all-male initiates in cavernous, underground chambers.

Finally you come to the 1st-century Roman house. In the brick-vaulted rooms of Titus Flavius Clemens' grand palazzo you can hear the sound of water rushing through ancient Roman pipes. Only the richest people could have running water in their homes.

Titus Flavius, cousin to the emperor, was a wealthy consul, one of the first in Rome to become a Christian. He had a secret room in his house where the Christian community could meet for clandestine worship when Christianity was illegal in Rome and its followers persecuted.

Pagan rites were banned in Rome in the 4th century and Christians often built churches over the previous temples. The altars of both later churches are placed directly above the altar of the Mithras temple.

The lower levels were discovered in 1857 by archaeologist Father Joseph Mullooly O.P., the then Prior of the Irish Dominican friars who have been custodians of the basilica since 1667. His book detailing the excavations is considered a classic in archaeology.

In an early example of recycling, there's a marble slab with a pagan epitaph on one side, later reversed and used for a Christian inscription. The pagan one is the most emotive: 'To the departed spirits: Marcus Aurelius Sabinus, also called The Little Rover. A most beloved child whose way of life outshone by far the young men of his own rank and age.'

There's no better place to get a feel for Rome's multi layered history.

BASILICA OF SAINT FRANCIS OF ASSISI, ASSISI

Perched on a ridge at the bottom of Assisi's medieval Old Town, the Basilica Papale di San Francesco is considered one of the spiritual and artistic highlights of Western civilisation. Dating from the 13th century and cited by UNESCO as 'an outstanding example of a type of architectural ensemble that has significantly influenced the development of art and architecture', this landmark church on two levels has welcomed pilgrims for centuries.

Construction of the basilica began in 1228 on the day St Francis was canonised, which was only two years after his

death in Assisi at the age of 44. Pope Gregory IX laid the first stone of what would become the 'mother house' for the Franciscan Order of Friars.

The Lower Church (Basilica inferiore), created to hold the saint's remains, was completed in 1230; the Upper Church (Basilica superiore) was ready for liturgical use in 1253. For the next twenty years, huge teams of artists came from all over Italy to paint the magnificent frescoes, among them the masters Giotto, Cimabue, Pietro Lorenzetti and Simone Martini. These frescoes are remarkable not only for their beauty; they bear witness to the unfolding of an artistic revolution in Italy.

In the 13th century an artist, long assumed to be Giotto but this since been disputed, broke away from the confines of the flat, two-dimensional style of medieval art to present a naturalistic approach, a development that would culminate in the Renaissance.

The most remarkable frescoes are on the walls of the Upper Church where serried ranks of panels narrate the history of Christianity. Being presented with two styles of art from the same period, seen side by side, is quite a revelation.

The earlier panels depicting Old Testament stories are painted in the Byzantine style of the period, with two-dimensional figures on plain, featureless backgrounds.

In contrast, Giotto's scenes from the lives of Christ and St Francis are filled with real people rooted in the real world. Here art is celebrating ordinary humanity in all its joys and frailties, showing familiar features and facial expressions. These figures move, feel and speak – to each other and to the viewer. In the background are buildings, trees and hills – many settings recognisably of Assisi – given the radical innovation of perspective. Such realism had never been seen before, nor had the harmony between God, man and nature been so depicted in art.

St Francis was born in Assisi around 1182, the son of a well-to-do cloth merchant. He enjoyed an affluent and boisterous lifestyle, nursing dreams of achieving military glory, then abandoned his worldly ambitions, giving away everything he possessed in order to imitate closely the life and work of Christ.

Francis taught by example, living in poverty, sleeping in fields, begging for food, aiming to love all of creation. In 1210 he founded an order of mendicant friars that became known as the Franciscans. His repudiation of the worldliness and hypocrisy of the decadent Papacy and his unassuming personality and humble lifestyle earned him a huge following.

By the mid-1400s pilgrims were arriving from all over Europe and the medieval town and its basilica is still one of the most visited Christian shrines. Despite the crowds, there's a surprising sense of peace about the church, the beauty and serenity of the frescoes adding to the air of tranquillity.

On completion of the Lower Basilica, the body of St Francis was brought from the church where it had lain since his death in 1228. Fearing that the remains might be looted, the actual burial site was kept secret and was only discovered in 1818. To house the relics, a crypt was carved out of rock beneath the lower church. Its interior was designed first in Neo-Classical style with marble, then renovated between 1925 and 1932 in a simpler, bare stone, neo-Romanesque style.

Lit by flickering candles, the air fragranced with incense, it emits an aura of peace. The simplicity reflects the life of the saint, who is entombed above a stone altar that rises like a pillar in the centre of the crypt. In the walls around the altar are the tombs of his four most faithful brothers-in-Christ and at the entrance, an urn bears the remains of his friend and benefactor Jacopa dei Settesoli, affectionately known as Brother Jacoba, whom he called to be with him at his death.

The Lower Church was designed originally to be the last resting place of St Francis and with its dim lighting and low Romanesque arches, it does indeed resemble a huge crypt. The frescoes depicting the Passion of Christ juxtaposed with the Life of St Francis, which cover the walls and ribbed vaults of the nave, are some of the oldest in the basilica.

As St Francis' fame grew, noble families commissioned side chapels. In the chapel built by an early 14th-century bishop of Assisi, Teobaldo Pontano, the superb paintings of Mary Magdalene, to whom the chapel is dedicated, are by Giotto or his workshop. Simone Martini's frescoes in the chapel dedicated to St Martin of Tours and in the St Elizabeth chapel are considered some of the finest examples of 14th-century painting.

In the right transept, Cimabue's *Our Lady Enthroned with St Francis* shows what is probably the closest known likeness of the saint. Giotto's lively panels nearby are a sharp contrast to Cimabue's beautiful but flat and static presentation. Masterworks by the Sienese painter Pietro Lorenzetti cover the left transept with a cycle of six monumental scenes from the Passion of Christ.

At the end of the nave, the papal altar from 1220 stands in the richly decorated, semi-circular apse. Featuring mosaics and delicate columns, it is fronted by two rows of walnut choir stalls carved with leaves, humans and animals on the armrests.

A doorway in the right transept leads to the Romanesque, 13th-century, friars' Chapter Hall where relics associated with St Francis, including his rough tunic patched with sackcloth, can be seen.

In contrast to the Lower Church, the Upper Church is light and spacious, with Gothic pointed arches, high, blue-painted ceilings and elegant stained glass windows. Alive with colour, it is a serene setting for the cycle of 28 frescoes that art aficionados have come here to see – Giotto's vivid depiction of events in the life of St Francis. Their realistic style, revolutionary at the time, marked a turning point in Italian art.

Thankfully they were not badly damaged in the devastating earthquakes that Assisi suffered in 1997. The basilica's vault collapsed, four people who were inspecting the damage were killed during an aftershock and a fresco by Cimabue was shattered into hundreds of thousands of fragments. Huge sums of money poured in from all over the world for its repair. The church reopened in 1999 and restorations continued into the new millennium.

Somehow, despite the crowds of visitors, *pax et bonum* (peace and goodness, the motto of St Francis) pervades this twin-churched basilica and its adjoining convent, majestically carved into the mountainside. All around, snuggling into woods and olive groves, are places that St Francis knew and loved.

CATHEDRAL OF MONREALE, SICILY

Framed by traditional Romanesque architecture, the Cattedrale di Monreale (official name Santa Maria la Nuova) and its cloister are masterpieces of Norman, Arab and Byzantine art. Shimmering mosaics cover every available surface, the artistry, detail and craftsmanship are extraordinary and the result is, quite literally, breathtaking.

Determined to outdo the cathedral in Palermo (and its bishop), the young Norman ruler King William II planned his own cathedral, together with a castle, abbey and bishop's palace, a few kilometres to the south at Monreale ('royal mountain'). He would exert his sovereignty in this spectacular display of regal wealth and power, aimed at bringing about a fusion of the main cultural traditions of the age: Western Latin, Eastern Orthodox and Arab-Islamic. Built between 1174 and 1189, it has come down the centuries relatively unscathed.

The statistics are mind-bending: 6,340 square metres (7,583 square yards) of wall space covered in mosaics made with 2,200 kilograms (4,850 lb or 2.2 tonnes) of pure gold. That it was completed in so short a time, and with such quality, is equally amazing.

With the exception of a 2-metre (6.5-foot)-high marble dado on the walls at ground level, brightly coloured glass mosaic figures interspersed with elaborate decorative patterns against a gold background cover all surfaces.

In a feast for the eye and the mind, tiers of panels comprising 130 'picture stories' reveal the whole history of the Christian religion, with explanatory inscriptions in Latin and Greek. They start from God's creation of the universe and end with the Apostles announcing the word of Christ and his Church to the world.

Norman architecture and Byzantine craftsmanship come together in the three-aisled nave. Two rows of nine columns in grey granite, except for one column in cream and green marble, crowned by richly carved Corinthian capitals, support ogival arches (a shape often found in Islamic architecture). Above this flight of arches, wall mosaics in the central nave depict scenes from the Old Testament, interspersed with large, light-giving windows. In the narrower side aisles and over the transept the mosaics follow the life, death and miracles of Jesus Christ. High above them all, the open roof truss is coffered, carved and beautifully painted.

The nave's 42 episodes cover the Creation and Adam and Eve in the Garden of Eden, through Cain and Abel, Noah and the Ark, the Tower of Babel, Abraham, Sarah and the visiting angels, the destruction of Sodom and Gomorrah and Abraham's sacrifice, ending in Jacob wrestling with an angel.

There are some wonderful expressions in the faces of these characters. Look for a depressed Eve seated on a rock while Adam toils in the background; the worried faces of Noah's family as he reaches out for the returning dove and the happy surprise of the eavesdropping Sarah as she learns she will after all conceive a child.

Such facial expressions, the sense of movement in the figures and action in the scenes, together with some clever indications of depth and perspective, are a notable transition from the previously more rigid style of Byzantine mosaic work.

A more pictorial art form does much to involve viewers in the stories and events they are following. This is particularly so as the life of Christ unfolds and in the stories of his miracles, from the curing of the blind and the sick to the raising of his friend Lazarus. There's no doubt about his anger as he upturns tables in the temple and drives out the traders; or the pain felt by his mother and followers at the crucifixion and the caring manner in which his body is laid in the tomb.

The Latin cross basilical plan of the building is clearly based on the Early Christian tradition while the triple-apsed choir and sanctuary has a distinctly Eastern influence.

Do take a look at its architecture from the outside, too. The three rounded apses are decorated with interlaced

ogival arches and inlaid with black lava in Arab-influenced geometric designs. The whole shows a symmetry that reflects Muslim spirituality.

Above the high altar, dominating the half-dome of the central apse, the monumental mosaic of Christ Pantocrator (the All-Powerful) is the focal point of the cathedral. In this huge image, over 13 metres (43 feet) across and 7 metres (23 feet) high, the bearded Christ is shown with outstretched arms, one hand raised in the Greek manner of blessing, the other holding an open book with the words 'I am the light of the world' inscribed in Greek and Latin. Surrounded by the most important members of his heavenly court and much symbolism, his penetrating gaze reaches you wherever you are in the cathedral.

Below, the Virgin Mary is depicted as the Theotokos (Mother of God) enthroned with the Christ child on her lap. Paying homage alongside her, the archangels Michael and Gabriel are joined by apostles and evangelists.

Illustrious churchmen are depicted on the lower level, including St Thomas Becket, the murdered Archbishop of Canterbury (page 18) who was canonised while the Monreale cathedral was under construction. It is one of the very earliest church depictions of the saint – and interesting as King William had quite recently married Joan, the daughter of King Henry II of England, the king complicit in Becket's murder. Full-length images of St Peter and St Paul, both enthroned, fill the other two apses, where wall mosaics present events from their lives.

Ensuring there was no doubt of his power and importance in the mind of the medieval viewer, above the king's throne in the sanctuary, King William II is shown being crowned by Christ. Over the bishop's throne he is seen giving a model of his Monreale church to the Mother of God. Also in the sanctuary are 12th-century tombs of Norman kings, and nearby the riches of the Cathedral Treasury are on display.

Although the mosaics are impressive to the naked eye, binoculars are a real asset here to get the full impact of the extraordinary detail in every panel.

The tranquil Benedictine cloister, too, is a space of pure artistry. Enclosing a garden square, the 26 elegant arches on each of the four sides are supported by sets of slender double columns topped by double capitals. No two pairs of columns are alike. Some are smooth, some swirly, some are boldly patterned, some inlaid with Byzantine-style mosaics. The capitals are alive with whimsical animals, exotic birds and mythical beasts, entwined plants, biblical scenes, Arab warriors and Norman knights, each one an individual and all carved in the finest detail.

Steps, (180 of them) and narrow passageways lead up to the cathedral's roof, where the terrace offers a bird's-eye view of the cloister and its manicured garden, the fertile surrounding valley, encircling mountains and out to sea.

– MALTA –

ST JOHN'S CO-CATHEDRAL, VALETTA

The plain façade of St John's Co-Cathedral (Kon-Katidral ta' San wann) gives no indication of the opulence within. Testimony to the wealth and importance of the Knights of Malta, the sheer ostentation of the flamboyant High Baroque decoration makes this a church unlike any other in Europe.

Photo: Sue Dobson

It was built in a mere five years, from 1573 to 1578, with the oratory and sacristy added in 1604, but the exuberant decoration came nearly a century later. The architect had trained as a military engineer and the severe appearance of the church reflected the decision of the knights, having defeated a fierce Ottoman attack known as the Great Siege, to turn their new capital into an illustrious fortress city.

The Order of the Knights Hospitaller of St John, a religious brotherhood, was founded in Jerusalem in the 11th century to care for pilgrims to the Holy Land. After the conquest of Jerusalem in 1099 during the First Crusade, they took on a military role. By the 16th century the mission of the knights, noblemen from some of the most important families in Europe, was to protect the Catholic faith and Europe from attack by the Ottoman Turks.

In 1530 the Holy Roman Emperor Charles V offered the Order the island of Malta as their base. After the Great Siege of 1565, the Grand Master Jean de Valette ordered a new defensive city to be built on a peninsula, to deter any future Turkish attacks. Valetta was founded just a few months after the siege ended in 1566; the Order's church, dedicated to their patron saint, St John the Baptist, would be at its heart.

The floor plan is simple: rectangular, with an apse at the east end and a wide nave of six bays flanked by two aisles divided into side chapels. When the highly decorative Baroque style became popular in Rome in the 17th century, the most famous artist of the time, Mattia Preti, was commissioned to give the interior of the church a Baroque makeover.

In the long, low nave, every wall, arch and rib is encrusted with gold carvings in a riot of foliage, flowers, cherubs and symbols of power, the columns being faced with the finest marble. The barrel-vaulted ceiling seems alive with action in Preti's scenes from the life of St John the Baptist among uplifting skies filled with angels. Around 400 multi-coloured, inlaid marble tombstones, individually designed and highly decorated to commemorate some of the most illustrious knights of the Order, cover the entire floor of the cathedral. The impact of so much gold, pattern and colour dazzles the senses.

Born in Calabria in 1613, Mattia Preti had spent years working in Italy where he'd been influenced by the work of Caravaggio, Veronese and Tintoretto. His powerful use of light and shade, the force and vigour of his figures and the sheer drama of his paintings are nowhere better revealed than in this cathedral. As well as decorating the vault, which he completed in just six years, he was also employed to prepare designs for the decoration of the church and commissioned to create altarpieces for some of the side chapels.

These eight chapels reflect the different 'langues' (regions) within the membership of the Knights of Malta. Even amid so much bravura, the Chapel of the Langue of Aragon stands out.

The burial place of four Grand Masters, its rich decoration includes a muscular painting by Mattia Preti of the valiant, dragon-slaying St George (the patron saint of the Aragonese knights, to whom the chapel is dedicated) astride a white stallion. The entrance arch is adorned with golden palms and laurels, the walls, too, are carved and gilded – look for the cherubs frolicking amid flowers, leaves and garlands.

Preti's superb altarpiece, *The Mystic Marriage of Saint Catherine*, is in the Chapel of the Langue of Italy, amid gilded carving and multi-coloured marble, fine sculptures, statues and paintings.

A ninth chapel, dedicated to The Virgin of Philermos, is where the knights went to pray before battle and hung the keys of captured fortresses on their return.

So much finery, so much detail to discover, so many symbols to decipher, and then there's the sanctuary, where the high altar, composed of lapis lazuli and rare marbles, glitters in gold and light-catching silver. In the choir stalls, 52 seats made from fine walnut wood and arranged in two tiers, have artfully carved gilt motifs. The pulpit, too, is an intricately carved work of art with gold detail, bearing all the attributes of a master craftsman.

Filling the apse, a golden sunburst of angelic carvings has the dove of the Holy Spirit casting rays on the two superbly executed figures below in *The Baptism of Christ by John the Baptist*, a masterpiece in marble by the leading 18th-century sculptor, Giuseppe Mazzuoli.

Entered from the back of the church, the ornate and gilded oratory is packed with important works of art. In pride of place and centre stage, *The Beheading of Saint John the Baptist* by Caravaggio is the cathedral's most famous and haunting painting. Dating from 1608, it is the largest work the artist ever painted, over 3 metres (12 feet) by 5 metres (17 feet) and the only one he ever signed. Here, too, you'll find one of Caravaggio's most recognisable works, *St Jerome Writing*, which was previously hung in the chapel of the Langue of Italy.

Adjoining the cathedral, the museum features rare, exquisitely illuminated choral books and manuscripts, precious relics, rich vestments and the largest complete collection of Flemish tapestries in the world.

Tradition required that when every new Grand Master was elected, he would offer a gift of high artistic value to the church. Based on drawings by Rubens and consisting of 29 pieces, the tapestries were the gift of the Aragonese Grand Master Ramon Perellos y Roccaful in 1701 and would have been suspended in the nave during important services, such as the feast of St John the Baptist. That's just one artistic example of the power, sophistication and wealth of the knights during their stay on Malta.

– NORWAY –

NIDAROS CATHEDRAL, TRONDHEIM

Topped by a distinctive green copper spire, Nidarosdomen stands rooted among trees near the mouth of the Nidelva (River Nid) in Trondheim. Nidaros was the ancient name for this city and former capital, founded by Viking King Olav Tryggvason as a trading post in 997.

Norway's national cathedral and symbol of the nation began as a wooden chapel erected over the tomb of St Olav, the Viking king who became the patron saint of Norway.

Born around the year 990, the son of a regional Viking chieftain in eastern Norway, Olav Haraldsson built a reputation as a mighty warrior in the Baltic and fighting with the Danes in England (who made a habit of burning down churches, including Canterbury Cathedral (page 18) in 1012 when they also murdered the archbishop). By following the English king Ethelred he ended up in Normandy, where he discovered Christianity and was baptised.

In 1015 he returned home a powerful and wealthy man, determined to unify Norway as an independent country and become its ruler, which he succeeded in doing seven years later, by means both fair and foul. Along the way he worked at converting pagan communities to Christianity, often by force.

By 1024 he had instituted a new Christian law, banning all heathen cults, and set up rule by absolute monarchy. But he didn't have it all his own way and Olav died in battle in 1030.

Miracles were alleged, a cult grew up around the king and he was canonised. A wooden church was erected over his burial site at the highest point on the shore of the River Nid, to be replaced by a stone church, which eventually developed into a cathedral, and with St Olav's shrine became an important pilgrimage destination.

St Olav is usually depicted either standing, axe in hand, or seated with a beast between his feet, symbolising the evil powers he overcame. The axe is his emblem and appears on the Norwegian coat of arms.

The building of a stone church began in 1070 and was completed in around 1300, having already been designated a cathedral in 1152. Dedicated to the Holy Trinity, in the Middle Ages it was known as Kristkirken (Christ Church).

It is partly Romanesque (the transept survives from this period) but mainly Gothic, thanks to a 12th-century Nidaros archbishop, Øystein Erlendsson, who on an enforced trip to England saw the latest styles in cathedral architecture.

When he returned three years later in 1183 he'd re-thought and revised the building plans for his own cathedral. The nave and choir bear a strong resemblance to Lincoln Cathedral (page 24) and the enormous Early Gothic octagonal sanctuary that he had built above St Olav's shrine is still a highlight for visitors today.

It was already the biggest building in Norway when in 1248 Archbishop Sigurd laid the foundation for a new nave extension, twice as long as the choir and ending in a wide façade: the west front.

A whole string of devastating fires down the centuries wrought major damage to the cathedral and often it was restored just enough to make at least parts of it usable. It was in a bad state of repair by the time of the Reformation in 1537, when St Olav's silver casket was taken to Denmark and melted down into coins. His remains were buried somewhere in the cathedral but have never been found. By the 19th century, the biggest church in Scandinavia and the world's most northerly medieval cathedral was practically a ruin.

Extensive restorations and faithful reconstructions were begun in 1869 and officially completed in 2001, although parts of the façade are again under repair currently.

The aim was both to restore Nidaros Cathedral to its medieval greatness and to create a magnificent west front that would stand as a symbol of Norwegian pride and identity as the country headed towards regaining its independence.

The ornate west front appears like an altar of sculptures, growing ever taller towards the top. Biblical characters, Norwegian kings and bishops all take their place here. Large numbers of sculptors and leading Norwegian artists were involved in this major project. Work was ongoing from 1905 until 1983, when the final statue, a copy of John the Apostle, one of only five medieval statues to survive, was put in place.

A winged sculpture of the Archangel Michael appears to have just landed on the top of the west front's north tower as he does battle with evil in the shape of a dragon. Completed in 1965, it is said that the sculptor used the musician Bob Dylan as his model for the angel's face.

Archaeologists found fragments of coloured glass during excavations in the 1990s, intimating that the original cathedral had stained glass windows. The current windows were created between 1908 and 1934.

The windows on the north side of the cathedral show scenes from the Old Testament against a blue background,

Photo: M. Heil

those on the south side are from the New Testament, on red. They start at the west end of the building with, respectively, the Creation and the Birth of Jesus and continue towards the high altar. The Apostles are under the vaulting of the choir and saints are found in the nave.

Glowing and vibrant, the great rose window depicts the Day of Judgement, with the red centre representing Christ. Flickering flames against a blue background radiate out towards cheerful musician angels, while the angels on the outside rim trumpet the warning that the end of the world is nigh. The nine windows below show Christ lining up the saved and the damned.

There are two principal altars, in the octagon and in the crossing. In the octagon, where the silver-gilt reliquary casket of St Olav once stood, the marble altar has been designed to represent the essential form of that casket. Amid powerful columns surging upwards, a modern silver crucifix, commissioned by Norwegian American emigrants in the early 20th century, dominates the crossing's altar. Groups of slim pendulant lamps drip from on high to light the cathedral's otherwise dim interior.

The early 14th-century altar frontal displayed in an ambulatory chapel is the most important artwork in the cathedral. Depicting scenes from the legend of St Olav, it is the earliest known representation of his life and one of the few things to survive from the Middle Ages.

In the crypt under the nave there's a collection of medieval tombstones. Mostly restored from fragments, many have inscriptions in Old Norse and Latin, some bearing carved portraits of the deceased.

Known as a centre for memorable music and hosting regular concerts and events, the cathedral boasts two great organs, including a Baroque instrument from the mid-18th century. Of the five resident choirs, one is an all-female Gregorian choir.

Norway's crown jewels and other treasures are on display next door in the Archbishop's Palace. The cathedral had long been the setting for the coronation of kings but three years after Norway's independence in 1905, coronations were abolished and replaced with blessings. When King Harold and Queen Sonia were blessed here in 1991, their crowns were placed on each side of the high altar.

In the summer (mid-June to mid-August) you can climb the 172 steps on the narrow spiral staircase of the cathedral's tower for great views over the attractive city.

The old pilgrim routes have been restored and now paths marked with St Olav's pilgrim symbol, all given the status of European Cultural Routes, lead through Sweden, Denmark and Norway to Trondheim, where the travellers are welcomed at the eighteen-room Nidaros Pilgrim Centre.

– POLAND –

CHURCH OF PEACE, ŚWIDNICA

In the countryside about 50 kilometres south-west of Wrocław, the little medieval town of Świdnica is the location of a surprising church. Set among woodland, the black and white half-timbered exterior of this Church of Peace (Ko ciól Pokoju) looks more like a Tudor mansion than a church.

It is the largest and most decorated of three churches built in the mid-17th century in the aftermath of the Thirty Years

War, a devastating religious conflict that ravaged swathes of Central Europe between 1618 and 1648. Under the Peace of Westphalia, which called for harmony and concord between Roman Catholic and Lutheran Europe, the Habsburg Holy Roman Emperor Ferdinand III allowed the Protestant communities in Lower Silesia to build a church in each of three towns: Głogów, Jawor and Świdnica. In deference to this 'act of tolerance' they were called Peace Churches.

However, strict conditions were imposed. The buildings must not resemble traditional places of worship – no steeples or bells were allowed – and they were to be built using only low quality materials such as wood, loam, clay and straw. Even nails were forbidden. They could only be erected outside of town (but within cannonball range of the city walls), must be paid for by the Lutheran communities themselves and, as if that wasn't enough, they had to be completed within one year.

Presumably the churches were not expected to last long, but an extraordinary architect and engineer, Albert von Säbisch, managed to create imposing buildings of structural complexity, two of which have survived down the centuries and are still in use. The first church to be built, at Głogów in 1651, was destroyed by a fire in 1758.

When the timber-framed, wattle and daub church at Świdnica was completed in 1657 after a mere ten months, it was the largest wooden church in Europe, accommodating up to 7,500 worshippers (3,500 seated). In 2001 it was inscribed in the UNESCO World Heritage List.

Unlike the plain simplicity of most Lutheran churches, the ornate and colourful interior of the Church of Peace is a bold celebration of the Baroque.

Laid out in the form of a Greek cross with a single nave, its walls are lined with two storeys of brightly coloured and gilded galleries, several small balconies and private boxes for the wealthy. The domed box of the Hochberg family, complete with their coat of arms, is particularly impressive, reflecting the generosity of Johann Heinrich von Hochberg of nearby Ksiaz Castle, who donated more than 2,000 tree trunks from his forest, two-thirds of the wood required to build the church.

Paintings cover the walls, galleries and ceiling with apocalyptic visions gleaned from the New Testament's Book of Revelation, a panorama of local towns, coats of arms of prominent members of the church community, the insignia of guilds representing butchers, brewers, tailors, drapers, glaziers and carpenters, biblical verses, portraits of townspeople and a whole host of angels playing a variety of musical instruments.

The gilded pulpit has an hourglass installed among the multitude of carvings that decorate it – a gentle reminder to over-enthusiastic preachers. Reliefs on the stairs depict the descent of the Holy Spirit, the Crucifixion and paradise. Topped by an angel trumpeting the Last Judgement, it was created in 1728.

Many of the sculptures in the church appear to be in marble but they were all carved from wood.

The altar is astonishing. Installed in 1752 to mark the centenary of the granting of permission to build the churches, the spectacular decoration alone took a year to create. The work of August Gottfried Hoffmann, a Dresden sculptor who had settled in Świdnica, its central scene depicts the baptism of Christ in the River Jordan, with a sunburst of the Holy Spirit shining light from above. The figures of Moses, Aaron and the Apostles Peter and Paul appear beneath an ornate canopy supported by six Corinthian columns. It towers on upwards in another

decorative tier to be crowned by a book with seven seals and a lamb bearing a banner.

Portraits of pastors from the church's 350-year history surround the multi-coloured wooden font in the Baptism Hall.

The baptism of the shoemaker's daughter was one of the first services to be held under the shingled roof of the church in June 1657. Worship has continued down the centuries, despite the wars and upheavals of history.

After the Second World War, under the Potsdam Agreement, Lower Silesia became part of Poland and its mainly Protestant German-speaking population either fled for their lives or were forcibly expelled. The Evangelical parish of the Holy Trinity in Świdnica dwindled from over 12,000 to around 100 faithful.

The church is still owned by this small Protestant community, which has a strong and active presence in the town. The annual International Bach Festival makes good use of the two restored 17th-century Baroque organs – the acoustics of the wooden church lend themselves particularly well to Bach's music. Art, sculpture and theatre workshops held here are highlights of the International Summer of Arts.

Several 300-year-old buildings and the cemetery that served the Protestant community for 250 years surround the church. Tucked away among trees, the bell tower was added in 1708.

The smaller Church of Peace at Jawor is about 30 kilometres away. Built a year before the church in Świdnica, although quieter in its decoration, the interior also resembles a theatre of the Baroque.

Painted predominantly in blue and white, worshippers are accommodated in four galleries painted with biblical scenes, with coats of arms and shields on the first level belonging to aristocratic families and guilds of the time. Throughout the church there are 180 paintings depicting scenes from the Old and New Testaments.

ST MARY'S BASILICA, KRAKÓW

Under a midnight blue ceiling spattered with stars, Kraków's brilliantly colourful Basilica of the Assumption of the Virgin Mary (Kościół Mariacki) is a joyous celebration of reverence to the Mother of God. Every inch of wall is painted and patterned in the rich tones of warm, welcoming colours, light filters through gloriously tall stained glass windows and gold glitters in the glow of candles lit by the faithful. A mix of the Gothic and the Baroque, it's a visual sensation.

The focal point and star attraction is a stunning winged altarpiece towering behind the high altar. This late Gothic masterpiece, a national treasure of Poland, was sculpted by the Nuremburg master carver Veit Stoss (known in Poland as Wit Stwosz) and built between 1477 and 1489. It is 13 metres (43 feet) high and 11 metres (36 feet) wide when open. Sculptures fill its centre section; reliefs decorate the four wings. The whole is dedicated to the Virgin Mary and her role in salvation.

On a frame of oak, with a background of larch, the scenes are carved from linden (lime) wood, painted in vibrant colours and gold leaf. Each one of the 2.7-metre (9-foot) tall lifelike figures is sculpted from an individual tree.

Depictions of the Dormition (Assumption) of the Virgin, who is surrounded by the twelve Apostles, fill the centre section. Hovering on the finial above, the figures of Poland's patron saints Stanislaw and Adalbert attend the Coronation of the Virgin Mary as the Queen of Heaven and Earth. The reliefs on the wings present eighteen scenes from the lives of Jesus Christ and His mother, Mary. The altarpiece is opened daily at a ceremony held at 11.50 am and on display until 5.30 pm (except on Saturdays when it is usually left open for the Sunday Masses).

Just before the German invasion of Poland, this precious work of art was dismantled, the statues taken to Sandomierz and the frame and wings hidden in different places around Kraków. However, intensive investigations by the Nazis led to its discovery and they shipped it off to Nuremberg, where the Allies recovered it from the vaults of the city's heavily bombed castle in 1946. After extensive restoration it was back where it belonged in St Mary's Basilica in 1957.

Of the dozen chapels within the church, the highlight is the Baroque Altar of the Holy Cross in black and pink marble, where a powerful stone cross by Veit Stoss is set against a silver background with scenes depicting Jerusalem.

Overlooking Kraków's magnificent Rynek Główny, the medieval main market square that's among the finest in Europe, St Mary's was built of brick on the foundations of a Romanesque church, and consecrated around 1320. Two square towers of unequal height dominate its plain façade. The taller tower, known as the Bugle Call Tower, has a gold crown ringing its main Gothic steeple; cupolas top the shorter tower, which houses the church bells.

Every hour, on the hour, a lone trumpeter signals the time from the four sides of the tallest tower. Known as the Hejnal Mariacki, this plaintive tune ends abruptly, as if in mid-flow. It's a tradition in memory of the unknown 13th-century bugler who, while trumpeting a warning of impending attack, was shot in the throat by a Tatar arrow. His signal allowed the gates of the city to be closed against the marauding horde. The noontime Hejnal is broadcast live on Polish national radio.

St Mary's is at the heart of Kraków's Old Town and countless churches all in close proximity throughout the city's centre reveal Polish architecture down the centuries. A tram-ride away in Nowa Huta district, however, there's a church that tells of more recent history and it's worth the short journey to reach it.

Built in the Communist 1960s, The Lord's Ark (Kościół Arka Pana) is symbolic of the determination and unwavering belief of the Polish people.

In the aftermath of the devastation of the Second World War, Nowa Huta was designed as a huge Socialist Realist suburb, a model city for 100,000 people and a fine example of social engineering. Funded by the Soviet Union, it had parks, wide boulevards and Socialist-design architecture. Churches were not part of the plan.

Volunteers built The Lord's Ark, mixing cement by hand, finding the 2 million stones needed for the building and carefully removing some 5,000 mines and shells after the discovery of an ammunition dump on the land. Cardinal Karol Wojtyła, later to become Pope John Paul II, laid the cornerstone in 1969 and the church was finally consecrated in 1977 after a decade of dedicated hard labour.

During the anti-communist protests of the early 1980s, a dangerous era when many lost their lives, the church became a gathering point. Built to resemble Noah's Ark, with a high mast-shaped crucifix rising from the centre, it contains some strange treasures, including a stone from the tomb of St Peter in the Vatican, a tabernacle containing a moon fragment brought back by the crew of Apollo 11 and a statue dedicated to Our Lady the Armoured, made from 10 kilograms (22 lb) of shrapnel removed from Polish soldiers

Photo: Jar.ciurus

injured during the Battle of Monte Cassino in 1944.

Such a contrast with fairy tale Kraków, a visit here makes an interesting foray into the recent past.

– PORTUGAL –

JERÓNIMOS MONASTERY, LISBON

Symbol of Portugal's power and wealth during the Age of Discovery and last resting place of explorer Vasco da Gama, the spectacularly ornate Mosteiro dos Jerónimos lines the bank of the Tagus River at Belém, a suburb to the west of Lisbon's city centre.

Prince Henry the Navigator built a chapel on this site near the mouth of the Tagus in 1460. Dedicated to Santa Maria de Belém, here seafarers prayed before launching out into the treacherous waters of the North Atlantic.

In 1497, Vasco da Gama spent the night in prayer there before leaving on an expedition that would lead to the discovery of the sea route to India. On his triumphant return two years later, King Manuel I ordered the building of a magnificent monastery and church in thanksgiving to the Virgin Mary for the explorer's success and safe homecoming.

Financed mainly from taxes levied on the spices and goods brought back from Africa, India and the Orient, construction of the three-aisled church began in 1502 and continued for about 100 years. Monks of the Order of St Jerome, a contemplative order known as Hieronymites, were invited to occupy the monastery, their role to pray for the souls of the king and his family and to provide spiritual assistance to the navigators and seafarers departing on long voyages of discovery. They stayed until late 1833 when monasteries were dissolved and the building appropriated by the state.

Built from local limestone and lavishly decorated, it is a triumph of the Manueline style of architecture, a combination of flamboyant Gothic, Moorish and Early Renaissance elements named in honour of the king.

Facing the river, the exuberance of the 32-metre (105-foot)-high south portal dazzles with its filigree-like stonework and 40-plus statues that include a bearded Prince Henry the Navigator, scenes from the life of St Jerome, prophets, saints and the twelve Apostles, watched over by the vigilant Archangel Michael. The central figure is Our Lady of Bethlehem (Belém), to whom the church is dedicated, holding gifts from the Magi in her hand.

King Manuel I and his second wife Queen Maria, together with St Jerome and St John the Baptist accompanied by angels and saints, preside over the smaller, but still impressive, main entrance to the Church of Santa Maria. Surmounted by groups of statues representing scenes from the birth of Christ – Annunciation, Nativity and the Adoration of the Magi – it is full of finely crafted filigree stone carving.

Vasco da Gama's ornate tomb, decorated with seafaring motifs, is to your left as you enter the church, opposite the revered 16th-century poet Luís de Camões, who extolled da Gama's discoveries in his epic poem *Os Lusíadas* (The Lusiads).

Six slim, elegant and deeply carved octagonal columns tower in the manner of palm trees, their tops branching out to form a complex web of lierne vaulting in a single span across the nave and two side aisles. Light streams through

Photo: José Carlos Cortizo Pérez

stained glass windows, their brilliant colours at their best on bright sunlit mornings.

The splendid tombs of King Manuel I and his Queen Maria, João III and Queen Caterina stand between columns in open arches on either side of the imposing high altar, each sarcophagus supported by pairs of glistening stone elephants. As the church became a pantheon for royalty, there are many family tombs to be found in the transept.

In a riot of decoration, everywhere you look there are elaborate sculptural details and maritime motifs; anchors, coiled ropes and navigational instruments, exquisitely wrought fish, seahorses, shells, coral and exotic plants.

The upper choir with its huge rose window offers a great vantage point for an overview of the church. The individually carved seats, early examples of the Renaissance style in Portugal, are where the monks spent several hours a day in prayer.

The honey-stone cloister, completed in the mid-16th century, is glorious. Quadrangular, it has two storeys of dazzling, intricately carved stone with tracery vaults; round, delicately scalloped arches and columns of intertwined vines. The crowning parapet is decorated with medallions portraying explorers, ships and Portuguese royalty, with ornamental bas-reliefs of fruits and plants from discovered continents.

Step from the cloisters into the former refectory, where a mosaic frieze of biblical scenes running right round the room seems a suitable backdrop to the monks' dinner. The west wing of the monastery, added in the mid-19th century, is home to the Maritime Museum and the National Archaeology Museum.

The monastery, church and cloister all serve as reminders of an extraordinary era when Portugal was a dominant maritime power whose ever-expanding empire stretched from Africa to India, Asia to South America.

– ROMANIA –

THE PAINTED MONASTERIES AND CHURCHES OF BUCOVINA

Romanian Orthodox monasteries scattered across the verdant valleys of Bucovina, a remote province in the north-eastern corner of Romania, stand out for the dramatic, brilliantly colourful frescoes that cover the exterior walls of their churches.

Dating from the 15th and 16th centuries, they were built under the rule of Stephen III of Moldavia (Stephen the Great), in an era when marauding Ottoman armies were a constant threat to the region. Depictions of battles often appear among the Biblical themes in an array of intensely coloured images that communicate their stories boldly across the countryside.

Stephen the Great, who ruled Moldavia from 1457 until his death in 1504, fought 36 battles against the Ottoman Empire, winning 34, and being a religious man he built churches after his victories. Eight of these churches, painted after his death, are now inscribed on the UNESCO World Heritage List. Today considered a national hero by Romanians, he was canonised in 1992.

The practice of painting on the exterior walls of the churches began in 1532 when Petru Rareş, illegitimate son of Stephen the Great and a prince of Moldavia who ruled from 1527 to 1538 and again from 1541 to 1546, ordered the decoration at the Monastery of Probota. Other, previously unadorned, churches in the region were inspired to follow suit and a new Orthodox tradition took shape.

With attacks and raids blighting life for centuries, poverty, squalor and illiteracy were deeply entrenched here. Painting the outside walls of churches offered the peasant farmers and soldiers visions of a living Christianity, a visual Bible with messages that could be understood by all.

Masterpieces inspired by Byzantine art, each painted monastery church is distinctive in architecture, colour and in its frescoed Bible stories, lives of saints and depictions of historical events. There are recurring themes, especially the Last Judgement and the Tree of Jesse, but no two representations are alike. Every inch of their interiors, too, is covered in wonderful frescoes.

The Church of St George at Voroneț, Romania's grandest monastery today taken care of by a community of nuns, is dubbed the Sistine Chapel of the East. Its size, the brilliance and intensity of its colours, the hundreds of figures, expressive faces and the beautiful detail in its frescoes are all remarkable. The distinctive blue colour used in the paintings, obtained from crushed lapis lazuli, is so special that artists worldwide know it as Voroneț Blue.

Built in 1488 by Stefan the Great to commemorate his significant victory over the Ottomans at the Battle of Vaslui, and in gratitude for the guidance of Daniil the Hermit, in 1547 the painting of its exterior walls was entrusted to the finest fresco painters of the time.

Given a vivid blue background, the entire western wall reveals an epic journey from the Garden of Eden to angels rolling up the zodiac, indicating the end of the world. The enormous Last Judgement has Christians rising from their graves, two by two, called by a trumpet-wielding, wonderfully winged angel. There are the nasties (Turks and Tatars in full killing cry) and the goodies (St Paul escorting believers to heaven).

Inside, equally spectacular if less intimidating frescoes fill every inch of the walls and cupola and long rows of icons stack up along the iconostasis.

One of the first to be painted and among the best preserved, the Church of the Assumption of the Virgin at Humor dates from 1530 under the rule of Petru Rareş, who is buried here, together with his wife. The monastery, which was closed by Habsburg forces in 1786, reopened in 1990 and today Humor is home to an order of nuns.

The predominant colour is a reddish-brown and its most important outside frescoes are 'The Return of the Prodigal Son' and the 'Hymn to Our Lady'. In the porch, images tell of what awaits the earthly sinner: fires (etched in red), eternal darkness (black) and the freezing cold (white) of hell. Elsewhere, St George slays the dragon and Satan is depicted as female.

There's a three-storey lookout tower to climb and enjoy the expansive country views.

In dazzling golds and deep blues, the Church of the Annunciation at Moldoviţa is spectacular. A procession of saints leads to the Virgin enthroned with the Child on her lap, while one wall is adorned with the intricate family Tree of Jesse, explaining the lineage of Jesus Christ depicted within the Holy Family.

The 'Siege of Constantinople' fresco is alive with cannons and horsemen marching up to towers and high walls. It tells the story of the Virgin's intervention in saving the city from Persian attack in the 7th century, but in a piece of pure political propaganda, the Persians are here portrayed as

Photo: Cristian Bortes

Photo: Raduachard

turbaned Turks. In the porch, a river of fire and a vision of the sea giving up its dead act as an awful warning.

Containing both Byzantine and Gothic elements, the Church of the Resurrection at Suceviţa Monastery was among the last to be built and decorated in the Moldavian style. It also took the longest to construct (from 1582 to 1601). Its colours are predominantly green and red and frescoes on one side are devoted to the Book of Revelation, depicting the Apocalypse in all its scary detail.

There's a fabulous Ladder to Paradise with hosts of red-winged angels attending the righteous while sinners fall through the ladder's rungs, to be met by grinning devils who escort them to a chaotic Hell.

Biblical episodes from both the Old and New Testaments cover interior and exterior walls. In a scene from the Garden of Eden, a coy Adam and Eve are provided with a whole bunch of fig leaves.

Sucevita was a princely residence as well as a fortified monastery and the large, square compound is surrounded by high, 3-metre (10-foot)-thick walls with a defensive tower on each corner. Among the monastic buildings, with around 50 nuns in residence, a good museum has ecclesiastical treasures alongside illuminated manuscripts that testify to Sucevita's history as a noted calligraphy and printing centre.

Less frequently visited, Arbore Church, built of brick and stone in 1503, is dedicated to The Beheading of St John the Baptist and named for its builder, the boyar Luca Arbore. Painting of the church took about 40 years and two heavy slabs of stone still outside the building have fifteen small holes that would have served as containers for mixing the colours.

The roof, which was originally made of lead, was plundered by marauding Cossack troops and turned into bullets, so the north side of the church has been badly affected by the elements and water damage.

The best-preserved frescoes, famous for their green colour, are on the south and west walls but, inside and out, stories unfold from the earliest Book of Genesis. The boyar and his large family are buried inside the tiny church and two votive paintings show them offering the church to God through the intercession of St John the Baptist.

The variety of the images and their stories makes each church fascinating. North-facing walls have suffered from the prevailing winds, rain and snow in Romania's tough winters and paintings have been faded by searing summer sun, but they are mostly in remarkably good condition, given that they've also survived hostilities – some bear the wounds of 19th-century graffiti left by Habsburg troops – and decades of neglect under Communism.

– RUSSIA –

HOLY TRINITY LAVRA, SERGIEV POSAD

Founded in 1337 by Russia's most revered saint, the monk Sergius of Radonezh, the Trinity Monastery of St Sergius (Troitse-Sergeiva Lavra) is the spiritual centre of the Russian Orthodox Church. A focus for pilgrimages for centuries, the city of Sergiev Posad (known as Zagorsk in Soviet times) is 75 kilometres (47 miles) north-east of Moscow and easily reached on public transport.

The most important working monastery in Russia began

Photo: Alex Zelenko

as a little wooden church dedicated to the Holy Trinity amid thick forest on Makovits Hill. The hermit St Sergius was in search of solitude but over time word of his piety and holiness spread and a monastic settlement grew up there.

Supported by the Princes of Moscow the monastery grew rapidly, becoming famous for producing chronicles, manuscripts and icons. Sergius died in 1392 at the age of 78 and was canonised as Russia's patron saint in 1422 – the year the Trinity Cathedral (Troitsky Sobor) was built to receive his relics.

Gleaming white, the golden-domed cathedral is lavishly decorated, the prayer-full atmosphere of the oil lamp-lit interior enhanced by the choirs who sing here all day.

Two of Russia's greatest icon painters, Daniil Chyorniy and Andrei Rublev were engaged to decorate the cathedral with frescoes. Repainted in the 17th century, these frescoes haven't survived but the iconostasis is still adorned with forty 15th-century icons. Rublev created his most famous icon, 'The Holy Trinity' ('Troitsa'), depicting three angels at a table, as the centrepiece of the iconostasis. The icon in the cathedral is a copy, the original being in the Tretyakov State Gallery in Moscow.

The subject of the Trinity was understood as a symbol of spiritual unity, mutual love and readiness to sacrifice oneself, which is why St Sergius chose it to dedicate his little church and ever-growing community of monks. Backed by rich icons, his majestic silver shrine in the Trinity Cathedral glitters under sanctuary lamps and glows in the light of flickering candles.

Surrounded by massive, multi-tiered, high, white walls and fortified by sturdy towers, the St Sergius Lavra is a town-sized complex of cathedrals, churches, chapels and monastery buildings where a panoply of golden onion domes and star-spangled blue cupolas gleam in the sunlight. It's a stunning spectacle.

With more than 50 buildings of different dates, the history of Russian architecture from the 15th to the 19th centuries is laid out within the walls of the lavra, which is home to over 300 monks, a theological college and an icon painting school.

You enter the monastery through an archway of the late 17th-century Baroque Gate Church of St John the Baptist, painted in warm ochre, passing frescoes telling of the life and work of St Sergius.

En route for the main cathedrals you pass the eye-catching and palatial Refectory, built by Tsar Peter I (Peter the Great) in 1692. Vibrant with colour and chequerboard patterning, its pillars elaborately carved with vine leaves and its porch dripping with white stucco moulding, it houses a chapel dedicated to St Sergius that's used in the coldest winter months when the Cathedral of the Assumption is closed.

Alongside it, in shades of peach-pink and prettily iced in white, the tiny Church of St Mica stands its ground against the vastness of its neighbour. It was erected in 1734 over the tomb of one of St Sergius' disciples.

The Refectory frames the central square of the monastery from the south. In the north is the equally massive and impressive Tsar's Palace. Painted the colour of sun-warmed sand and elegant in finest Moscow Baroque style, it provided a suitable resting place for the nobles who were constant visitors.

At the centre of the complex, the beautiful Assumption Cathedral (Uspensky Sobor) has four dazzling blue domes adorned with light-catching gold stars and crosses surrounding a central gold dome. Commissioned by Tsar Ivan IV (the Terrible) and based on the Dormition Cathedral in Moscow's Kremlin, but bigger, it took 26 years to build and was completed in 1585. The frescoes came a century later. Created in 100 days by a team of 35 painters from Yaroslavl, they cover the walls, pillars and vaults, a surface area of 500 square metres (598 square yards).

The magnificent five-tier iconostasis consists of 76 icons from the 16th and 17th centuries and features the Icon of 'The Last Supper', a masterpiece by Simon Ushakov, a favourite of the Tsar Alexei.

Tsar Boris Godunov has a family mausoleum here, the only tsar not to be buried in Moscow's Kremlin or the Cathedral of Saints Peter and Paul in St Petersburg. His death in 1605 plunged Russia into the Time of Troubles, a decade of war and jockeying for political power, during which the monastery suffered a sixteen-month siege by an army of 30,000 Polish-Lithuanian invaders and heroically prevailed.

The missionary priest St Innocent is buried in the cathedral. A man of huge talent, he founded the Russian Orthodox community of Alaska and is known as the 'apostle to America'.

A two-headed eagle is a reminder that the future Peter the Great twice found refuge here. It was his daughter, the Empress Elizabeth, who gave the monastery the status of Lavra, the highest rank of Orthodox monasteries (there are only four in the whole of Russia) in 1744. In 1782, Catherine the Great had the area surrounding the lavra reorganised to form the town of Sergiev Posad.

More must-see churches include The Descent of the Holy Spirit upon the Apostles, a graceful, single domed church erected in 1476 by master builders from Pskov and one of the few remaining examples of a Russian church topped by an open bell tower. Nearby, the pretty Chapel Over the Well was built over a spring discovered in 1644, and is always crowded with believers filling their bottles with the holy water considered to have healing powers. Its colourful tent-like domed canopy, faced with golden yellow walls and decorated in dark green with a gold spire, was built in 1872.

Watching over them all, painted in turquoise and iced in white, the elegant, five-tiered, 18th-century Baroque bell tower topped in shimmering gold houses 26 bells, one being the biggest working bell in Russia.

Under the Bolshevik government, in 1920 the lavra was closed and while it physically survived as a historical and architectural museum, the monks were dispatched to labour camps. In 1930 the city of Sergiev Posad was renamed Zagorsk, in honour of a former Bolshevik revolutionary assassinated in 1919.

As part of the victory celebrations after the Second World War, Joseph Stalin allowed the lavra to function again in 1946, when it became the seat of the newly established patriarch of Moscow and All Rus. The city regained its name in 1991 and the lavra was included in the UNESCO World Heritage List in 1993.

Sergiev Posad claims to be the birthplace of the *matryoshka*, the ubiquitous Russian nesting doll, and there's no shortage of supply in the souvenir market on the square near the monastery gate.

CATHEDRAL OF CHRIST THE SAVIOUR, MOSCOW

On the northern bank of the Moskva River in sight of the Kremlin, the Cathedral of Christ the Saviour (Khram Krista Spasitela) is the tallest Orthodox cathedral in the world. In brilliant white marble and red granite with four gold-capped towers set around a central gleaming gold dome, its majestic exterior is a landmark in this city of churches, cathedrals and monasteries. Inside it's a breathless world of colour and glittering gold. Consecrated at the turn of the new millennium, a symbol of revival and hope, this is the story of the church that would not die.

After the retreat of Napoleon's troops from Moscow in December 1812, Tsar Alexander I declared his intention to build a cathedral in gratitude to God for saving Russia and to honour the victorious Russian army. He would dedicate it to Christ the Saviour.

Alexander died of typhus before construction got under way on the Sparrow Hills overlooking the city (subsequently crowned by a white skyscraper in a style of architecture dubbed 'Stalin wedding cake'). His successor, his reactionary younger brother Nicholas I, disliking the design, called in his own favourite architect, Konstantin Thon, whose work included grand buildings in the Kremlin.

Taking as his model the Hagia Sophia in Constantinople (page 218), the new plan for the cathedral called to mind the ancient Russian churches built in the Byzantine style. A medieval convent and church that stood on his chosen site on the Moskva River embankment near the Kremlin was cleared away so construction could begin in 1839. The scaffolding came down in 1860, leaving some of Russia's finest painters to spend the next twenty years working on the elaborate frescoes.

At the suggestion of his friend and mentor Nikolai Rubinstein, Tchaikovsky wrote his *1812 Overture* to be performed at the new cathedral and for the All-Russia Arts and Industry Exhibition of 1882. Rubinstein's intention was for a grand commemorative piece to glorify the defeat of the French troops and the valour of the Russian people.

Tchaikovsky followed the brief with a heart-tugging mix of soulful hymns and patriotic Russian folk songs, the theme of *God Save the Tsar* drowning out strains of *The Marseillaise*. He wrote it in six weeks and hated it.

In the event it was performed in a tent outside the still unfinished building a year before the cathedral was consecrated in 1883 for the coronation of Tsar Alexander III.

The Russian Revolution of 1917, and the chaos that followed it, changed everything. By the late 1920s the Soviet government in Moscow had other ideas for this prime site by the river. They planned a grandiose Palace of Soviets, taller than the Eiffel Tower and topped by a gigantic statue of Lenin, outdoing New York's Statue of Liberty in size, as a symbol of socialist victory.

The cathedral was closed, its gold melted down, its treasures dispersed and its marble recycled to decorate new Metro stations. Joseph Stalin ordered the demolition to begin in December 1931 and the cathedral was dynamited into history. It took a year to clear the site.

Its replacement was never built. Though the foundations for it were laid, lack of funds, the river overflowing its banks, and then the outbreak of the Second World War all put a brake on building. The gigantic hole blighted the cityscape until 1958, when Nikita Khrushchev's planners had the idea of turning it into the world's largest public outdoor heated swimming pool. For many visitors the sight of steam rising into the dark, cold winter air seemed symbolic of Soviet-era Moscow.

Then times changed again, perestroika launched a very different kind of Russian revolution and in 1990 Patriarch Alexei II received permission for the Russian Orthodox Church to build a new Cathedral of Christ the Saviour, replicating the design of the original that had stood on the site.

Funded by church, city government, banks and a million

Photo: Voytek S

Muscovites, construction began on the $360 million building in 1994. More than 2,500 people worked in shifts around the clock, seven days a week, to complete the cathedral for its consecration in August 2000. It is vast. Accommodating 10,000 people, it fills to capacity at Christmas and Easter.

Beneath the main building, amid a plethora of administrative offices, the underground Church of the Transfiguration commemorates the 16th-century church that stood on this site. It has three altars and contains an icon that somehow survived from the destruction of the original cathedral.

From the great bronze entrance doors, fine statues of saints and reliefs depicting battle scenes from the war of 1812 to the brilliantly (some would say garishly) coloured, fresco-filled and gilded interior, its decoration encapsulates Russia's history. The last Romanov Tsar, Nicholas II, and his family achieved sainthood when they were canonised here in 2000.

ST ISAAC'S CATHEDRAL, ST PETERSBURG

The grand and glorious city of St Petersburg isn't short of cathedrals. Churches were as important as palaces in showing off the wealth and power of the rulers in what was then the capital of the vast Russian Empire. The best architects and artists were employed and no expense was spared in their construction. Their restoration since the fall of communism has been equally impressive. With over 200 churches in St Petersburg, there always seems to be a spire or a cupola in your sightline as you walk the city streets.

The needle-slim golden spire of the Cathedral of Saints Peter and Paul spikes the sky above the Peter and Paul Fortress. Nearly all the rulers of Russia since Peter the Great have found their last resting place here. The graves of Tchaikovsky, Dostoevsky and a host of Russian cultural celebrities are found amid the vast complex that is the evocative Alexander Nevsky Monastery, with the Holy Trinity Cathedral at its heart.

Multi-coloured onion domes define the ornately decorated, canal-side Cathedral of the Saviour on the Spilled Blood. Said by its restorers to contain more mosaics than any other church in the world, it is the go-to, gawp-at museum. There's the dazzling blue and white Baroque exterior of Smolny Cathedral to see and the pretty pink and white Cathedral of St Andrew the First Called, an active church that's an essential sight on Vasilevsky Island.

On the Petrograd side of the city, the lovely Prince Vladimir Cathedral isn't on the usual tourist route but it is quite near the Peter and Paul Fortress and worth seeking out. Except for the one year it was closed in 1926, it functioned during the communist years when churches and cathedrals were torn down, turned into museums or used as warehouses (one church on Nevsky Prospekt had its inside dug out for a swimming pool).

The popular Transfiguration Cathedral, all lemon and white, surrounded by cannons and set in a pretty square, also kept going during Soviet times. As did my personal favourite, the turquoise, white, gold and gloriously Baroque Naval Cathedral of St Nicholas. On the banks of the Kryukov Canal near the Mariinsky Theatre, it has an upper and a lower church and icons that were a gift from Catherine the Great.

With its outstretched wings of curving stone colonnades, the 19th-century Cathedral of Our Lady of Kazan dominates

Photo: Zemlyanichka

a whole block of St Petersburg's legendary main boulevard, Nevsky Prospekt. Modelled on St Peter's Basilica in Rome, its huge bronze doors a copy of those on the Baptistry in Florence, it houses a popular icon and is always busy. Closed for services by the Bolsheviks, it survived the Soviet years as the Museum of the History of Religion and Atheism, and reopened for services in 1992.

Since 1990, St Isaac's Cathedral (Isaakievskiy Sobor) has combined its main role as a state-run museum with offering daily services at a side altar, reserving its main altar and its massive central space, which can accommodate 14,000 worshippers, for major religious occasions. It was packed when the 2016 Christmas Eve liturgy was celebrated there for the first time since the church was closed in 1928. (Stripped of its ecclesiastical treasures, it reopened as a state historical museum in 1931.)

Originally the city's main church and the largest cathedral in Russia, St Isaac's was 40 years in the building and the life's work of its young Parisian chief architect, Auguste de Montferrand, who only lived for a further six weeks after its completion in 1858.

Before the foundations could be laid, in order to stabilise the construction of such an immense monument, over 10,000 tree trunks were driven into St Petersburg's boggy marshland, to a depth of 6 metres (20 feet) and then topped by a compacted layer of stone to the depth of 7 metres (23 feet). Half a million people were involved in the cathedral's creation and hundreds of serfs lost their lives during the construction process.

Vast and imposing, this Neo-Classical city landmark in grey and pink granite hauled in from Finland, has four colonnaded façades, all equally impressive, and a spectacular dome, gilded with over 100 kilograms (220 lb) of pure gold, that's visible for miles around. The dome's innovative design later influenced the dome of the United States Capitol Building in Washington, DC.

Ornately sculpted bronze bas-reliefs and statues of angels, apostles and saints decorate the building – there are 24 angels and archangels on the dome's balustrade alone. The rotunda's encircling walkway and observation deck are a big tourist attraction and the view out over the city is magnificent, well worth the 262-step climb.

Inside, the decoration is overwhelming and the statistics for the construction materials hard to grasp: 408 kilograms (900 lb) of gold, sixteen tonnes of malachite, 499 kilograms (1,100 lb) of lapis lazuli and 1,000 tonnes of bronze. Fourteen different kinds of marble were used for the arches, panelled walls, huge pillars and the intricately patterned floor.

Six columns of green malachite and two of lapis lazuli frame the three-tiered iconostasis that itself frames a brightly coloured stained glass window (unusual in an Orthodox church) depicting the resurrected Christ.

When the original wall paintings began to deteriorate in the cold, damp air of St Petersburg, Montferrand ordered them reproduced as mosaics. It was a hugely time-consuming and laborious process so it became a task that was never quite completed.

The announcement in January 2017, that the running of St Isaac's Cathedral was to be handed over to the Russian Orthodox Church, created much local controversy. Opponents feared restricted access and loss of funds for maintenance – the cathedral attracts over 2.5 million visitors a year and much of their entrance fee goes into the upkeep of the building. Under church rather than museum rules, entry fees would be scrapped. Critics of the decision aren't convinced that the Church will invest the millions of roubles required each year for the near-constant renovations and are concerned for its future care.

– SPAIN –

LA SAGRADA FAMILIA, BARCELONA

A triumphant, surreal and exuberant vision of faith and nature, Antoni Gaudí's unfinished masterpiece, the Basílica i Temple Expiatori de la Sagrada Familia, engages all the senses.

Gaudí's concept for the Sagrada Familia was based on the traditions of Gothic cathedrals. In the shape of a Latin cross, with a central nave, aisles and transepts, the top of the cross being capped by a semi-circular apse, it was rooted in tradition but grew into something unprecedented.

Nature and the Christian message guided his work. Taking inspiration from the Scriptures and liturgy and his observations of the natural world, Gaudí applied nature's forms and functions to his own brand of architecture. A snail's shell informed his staircases, seen as a link spiralling between earth and heaven; in the nave, double twisted columns branch, tree-like, into a vault of leaves. You feel at the heart of a towering stone forest. Everything seems designed to draw your eye upwards.

The dizzying vertical lines of the building signify elevation towards God, whose symbol Gaudí saw as light – and light he brings in abundance. It flows through coloured glass that bathes the great spaces with dappled rainbow patterns; in the skylights between columns, gold and green glass and tiles are used to reflect daylight inside. In the apse, the graduated shades of the glass create an atmosphere for introspection.

Outside, the rising sun lights up the portals of the elaborately ornate Nativity façade, much of it completed by Gaudí himself; the rays of the mid-day sun warm the main entrance that will represent the road to God, while the light and shade of the setting sun highlight the austere character of the Passion façade, where the haunting features of gaunt figures express the cruelty of Christ's final hours on earth.

Gaudí considered colour to be an expression of life and he uses it in all its brilliance, in stained glass windows, in Venetian glass mosaics and enamelled ceramics. It glistens on pinnacles and crowns towers and rooftops. Even in the nave's 'forest' the columns vary in colour from the soft Montjuïc stone through to granite, dark grey basalt and red-tinged porphyry.

The three monumental façades represent crucial Christian beliefs – Christ's Nativity, his Passion, Death and Resurrection, and his Celestial Glory (which when it is completed will be the main entrance and have seven doorways into the nave). The design of each façade is unique, linked only by the portals of each being covered in sculpted figures, tableaux-like, in scenes of events told in the Gospels.

Of the eighteen planned towers, the central tower is dedicated to Jesus Christ and the four towers around it represent the Gospels. Above the apse, the tower crowned by a star is for the Virgin Mary, the remaining twelve towers signifying the Apostles. When completed, the Jesus tower will be 172 metres (565 feet) tall, one metre shorter than the peak of Montjuïc, Barcelona's mountain, respecting Gaudí's belief that no man-made creation should top that of God's.

Symbolism is everywhere. Loaves, ears of corn and grapes

Photo: Sagrada Família (oficial)

represent the bread and wine of the Eucharist. Turtles supporting columns symbolise time set in stone; chameleons are all about change. In an abundance of flora and fauna, the fertility of nature heralds the birth of the Saviour; white doves (souls of the faithful) find sanctuary in a cypress tree (immortal life). The fruits that crown pinnacles signify good works, those resembling grasses tell of the sublime heights of religion. Molluscs, amphibians and reptiles replace traditional gargoyles.

Born in Reus in 1852, at school Gaudí excelled in geometry and learned about crafts in his coppersmith father's workshop. He worked in an architectural practice and as an assistant to a carpenter, a glassmaker and a locksmith while studying at Barcelona's School of Architecture, where design, drawing and mathematical calculation proved to be his forte.

Gaudí was working on other assignments in 1883 when he took over the design of the Sagrada Familia on the site of a neo-Gothic project begun a year earlier. By the time the crypt was finished in 1889, he'd decided to replace the neo-Gothic plan with a new, grander design, monumental in its scope, innovative in its construction.

The foundations for the Nativity façade were laid in 1892. In 1914 he left all other work to concentrate on what would become an obsession until his death at the age of 74 in 1926, when he was hit by a tram while crossing the road. He was buried in the crypt's Chapel of Our Lady of Mount Carmel.

The large crypt with its sturdy stone columns, pointed arches and chapels feels very traditional and restrained; the simplicity of Gaudí's tomb fits in perfectly here.

In 1936, revolutionaries set fire to the crypt, destroyed Gaudí's studio workshop holding his notes and designs, and smashed large-scale plaster models. After the Spanish Civil

War ended, work resumed using the restored models (it took sixteen years to piece one together), photographs and published designs to ensure continuity with the architect's original plans. Since then a series of architects have attempted to continue his legacy. An on-site museum has drawings and scale models showing the construction process.

In 2010, Pope Benedict XVI consecrated the Sagrada Familia and raised it to the status of basilica. The goal for 2020 is to finish all six central towers and the aim is for the building to be completed by 2026, for the centenary of Gaudí's death. After that, count on a further four to six years to work on more decoration.

From the very start its construction and upkeep have been funded by donations, boosted in the last few decades by the money received from tourist entrance fees. It may still be a work in progress, but an estimated 3 million people visit every year.

SEVILLE CATHEDRAL, SEVILLE

From its foundations as the Great Mosque when Seville became the capital of the Almohad Empire in 1170 to its construction as the biggest Gothic church in the world in the 15th century, Seville's cathedral (Catedral de Santa María de la Sede) has much to boast about.

Its sheer size and grandeur are overwhelming. Packing in 80 side chapels, it has the extraordinary tomb of Christopher Columbus, paintings by Murillo, Goya and Zurbarán, the world's largest altarpiece, church treasure galore – and a stuffed crocodile.

Photo: Sue Dobson

There are remnants of the 12th-century Almohad Mosque: the bronze-plated door leading into the Patio de los Naranjos (Orange Tree Court) decorated with minute Moorish images and religious inscriptions in Kufic script and the Puerto del Lagarto (Lizard Door) renowned for its fine Mozarabic vaulting. Most famously it is the minaret, converted into a bell tower known as La Giralda, which everyone remembers.

After King Ferdinand III's conquest of Seville in 1248, the mosque was adapted for Christian worship and consecrated as the Cathedral Church of Santa Maria. By the early 15th century the mosque was in bad shape and the decision was made to raze it and build a stone cathedral in the Gothic style, 'so magnificent that those who see it will think we are mad' (the church elders are said to have exclaimed).

Flanked by double aisles, with chapels leading off between the buttresses, the extremely long nave has a simple elegance with tall, slender pillars. In clusters resembling bunches of reeds, they rise to a neck-cricking height into austere cross vaulting. That simplicity is in sharp contrast to the opulence displayed when you explore further into the building – after all, this cathedral was built (from the 1400s to 1506, plus later additions) to demonstrate Seville's wealth and influence.

The Capilla Mayor (Main Chapel) certainly does that. Surrounded by three tall and intricately designed gold *rejas* (screens) in High Renaissance style, it is dominated by a 20-metre (66-foot)-high altarpiece of polychromed wood smothered in gold. With 44 carved scenes from the life of Christ, various saints and Old and New Testament scenes set around the Virgen de la Sede, the cathedral's patron saint, it contains over 1,000 biblical figures. This masterpiece of Gothic carving is considered the largest and richest altarpiece in the world.

Filling the central part of the nave, the Choir is enclosed in spectacular style by a decorated gold *reja* adorned with a Tree of Jesse showing the genealogy of Christ. Two tiers of Gothic choir stalls, carved from ebony during the 15th century, have misericords straight out of a medieval bestiary. The backs of the upper stalls are decorated with exquisite lace-like carvings and Mudéjar motifs.

Dating mostly from the 15th and 16th centuries, the 75 magnificent stained glass windows that illuminate the cathedral's vast interior are themed to depict saints, apostles, martyrs, evangelists and events in the life of Christ and the Virgin Mary.

The elliptical ground plan of the light and lovely Sala Capitular or Cabildo (Chapter House) was way ahead of its time in 1558. Described by UNESCO as 'one of the most beautiful architectural works of the Renaissance', its coffered dome ceiling soars heavenwards above a complicated *trompe l'oeil* marble floor based on a design by Michelangelo. Murillo's masterwork *La Inmaculada* hangs high above the Archbishop's chair.

Under the finely carved stone dome of the Sacristía Mayor (Main Sacristy) are two of the cathedral's most precious paintings: Pedro de Campaña's *Descent from the Cross* and Francisco de Zurbarán's *Santa Teresa*. Among the eye-watering treasure is a huge (475-kilogram/1,048-lb) silver processional monstrance, made in the 1580s by the Renaissance metalsmith Juan de Arfe. Look, too, for the keys presented to Ferdinand III by the Moorish and Jewish communities when they surrendered the city to him.

An abundance of art treasures, from paintings to opulent tombs and stunning altarpieces, inhabit the side chapels. The Capillo de San Antonio houses the enormous canvas depicting the vision of St Anthony of Padua by

Murillo (1656); Goya's painting of the Seville martyrs Justa and Rufina hangs above the altar in the Sacristy of the Chalices.

In the lavishly adorned Capilla Real (Royal Chapel) a spectacular Baroque silver gilt shrine, a masterpiece of the goldsmiths' art, holds the relics of the canonised Ferdinand III. In the crypt below there's a 13th-century ivory statue of the Virgin and Child that, tradition says, the king carried during his battles with the Moors.

Four bearers representing the kingdoms of Castile, Leon, Aragon and Navarra support the monumental tomb of Christopher Columbus, whose bones seem to have travelled almost as far as he did in life.

He died in poverty in Valladolid in northern Spain in 1506. After being interred in that city, his bones were transferred to a monastery in Seville before being moved to the West Indies, to Santo Domingo (where his son had been governor) in the mid-16th century. In 1795 they were transported to Havana, finally to return to Seville from Cuba in 1898.

While the exterior is richly carved, especially around the many entrance doors, unlike most cathedrals Seville's presents its face to the world without great towers or domes. Its long rectangular shape comes from its building on the footprint of the original mosque.

The Patio de los Naranjos, a large courtyard planted with orange trees inhabited by twittering birds (glorious when the blossom is out in spring) is where Moorish worshippers would have performed their ablutions before entering the mosque to pray. The octagonal fountain at its centre is an original from the Visigoth period.

That stuffed crocodile hangs in one corner of the Patio. It was a gift to King Alfonso X in 1260 from the Sultan of Egypt who wished to marry his daughter. The wedding never took place but the crocodile stayed and was stuffed (the one you see today is a replica).

A series of ramps, built for guards to ride up on horseback, go all the way to the top of the Giralda, the 12th-century minaret that survived to become the cathedral's bell tower. Its delicate geometric and latticed brick-pattern decoration is topped by 16th-century Christian additions and the bronze weathervane, El Giraldillo. This figure of a female bearing a cross to represent faith is a symbol of the city. It's a long climb, but there's a dazzling view from up there.

– TURKEY –

HAGIA SOPHIA, ISTANBUL

One of the great buildings of the world, the religious focus of the Byzantine Empire and for nearly 1,000 years the biggest church in Christendom (until the completion of Seville's cathedral in the early 16th century, page 213), the story of Hagia Sophia (Ayasofya, Church of Holy Wisdom) spans Orthodox Christian church, Imperial Ottoman mosque and a museum visited by millions.

Built by the Emperor Justinian I between 532 and 537, over the ruins of earlier basilicas from the time of Constantine the Great, the first Christian emperor, no expense was spared in the creation of what would come to be considered the ultimate symbol of Byzantine architecture. The best builders and craftsmen were brought from all over the empire; marble was sourced from temples and ancient sites including Athens, Rome, Baalbek, Pergamum, Ephesus and Delphi.

Greek architects and mathematicians Isidorus of Miletus and Anthemius of Tralles were chosen for the momentous design task and around 10,000 men were employed for the five years and ten months of its construction.

They came up with some daring engineering feats in the 6th century and architects are still marvelling at their innovations. A technically complex system of vaults and semi domes, arches, arcades, piers and galleries culminates in the massive shallow dome that's 31 metres (102 feet) in diameter. The 40 windows at its base give the impression that it is floating in air.

Almost 1,500 years since it was built, few visitors are able to hide the sense of awe they experience when stepping into that vast, airy space.

In the centre of the great gilded dome, a passage from the Koran is inscribed in gold around an image of a sun. The apse blazes with the glorious gold mosaic of the Madonna and Child; above the door once reserved for the emperor, Christ Pantocrator, Ruler of All, full of power and majesty, raises a hand in benediction. In the south gallery, Christ is depicted between the Empress Zoe and her husband, Constantine IX and the Virgin is shown with the Emperors Justinian and Constantine I.

Above the exit gate, a fine mosaic shows the Virgin Mary and Child Jesus at the centre with, on the right, Constantine the Great presenting them with a model of the city he founded and to the left, the Emperor Justinian offering a model of the church he built, the Hagia Sophia. It probably dates from the 10th century.

In 1204 the church was attacked, desecrated and looted by Crusaders, led by the Doge of Venice. They had set out for the Holy Land but considered the treasures of St Sophia easier to access, and they proved correct. They ousted the Patriarch and for 57 years Constantinople was the capital of the Latin empire. The Treasury of St Mark's Basilica in Venice holds more of Ayasofya's riches than can be seen in Istanbul.

It remained a functioning church until 1453 when Sultan Mehmet II The Conqueror triumphed over the city and immediately had the Hagia Sofia converted into his imperial mosque, plastering over the mosaics, replacing Christian furnishings with Islamic decoration and adding four minarets.

It served as a principal mosque of Constantinople for almost 500 years, with changes and additions by successive sultans along the way, and influenced the design of many religious buildings for centuries. The revolution of Kemal Attatürk transformed Turkey into a secular state and in 1934 the mosque became a museum.

Many of the glorious mosaics were vandalised by the Crusaders, some were destroyed by earthquakes and those that remained were hidden behind whitewash and plaster under the Ottomans. During a major two-year renovation in 1847, mosaics in the upper gallery were exposed and cleaned (and covered up again). The massive Islamic medallions hanging on pillars around the nave, the work of the greatest calligrapher of the 19th century, date from this renovation. Today, as well as getting visitors close to the mosaics, the galleries offer a fabulous view of the nave and interior of the mosque with its *minbar* and *mihrab*.

The condition of the building had deteriorated badly by the time it was closed for worship and opened as a museum. More mosaics were uncovered in the late 1930s, and grants from the World Monuments Fund saved the dome from potential collapse during renovations carried out between 1992 and 2006. There is still work to be done on what is now the most visited museum in Turkey.

Photo: Jorge Láscar

– UKRAINE –

MONASTERY OF THE CAVES, KIEV

Since its foundation in 1051, the Pechersk Lavra (Monastery of the Caves) has been an important centre of Eastern Orthodox Christianity and a place of pilgrimage for centuries.

Clinging to forested hills sweeping down to the wide Dnieper River, within its fortified walls lie a multitude of cathedrals, churches, bell towers, monasteries, museums, a theological college and seminary, and two complex underground cave systems where chapels and tombs punctuate the narrow passages.

Burned, invaded, raided, fought over, sacked and secularised, its history is long and turbulent. After each setback, the monastery was rebuilt, new churches were added and the underground tunnels, caves and catacombs expanded. It became a noted centre of learning, producing chroniclers and fine icon painters from a studio founded in the 11th century. The first printing press in Kiev was established here in 1615.

A great fire in 1718 damaged most of its buildings and destroyed the library and archive. The restoration that lasted ten years resulted in much of the Ukrainian Baroque architecture seen today. By this time the monastery had become hugely wealthy, owning cities, towns and villages, brickyards, foundries, factories, farms, mills, 70,000 serfs, numerous distilleries and 200 taverns.

There were over 1,200 monks and novices at the monastery before the Russian Revolution of 1917 changed everything.

One of the most famous centres of Orthodox religious life, it attracted hundreds of thousands of pilgrims. In 1921, the Soviet authorities confiscated relics and treasure and turned buildings into museums. The monastery was closed down completely in 1926 and the grounds turned into a state museum-preserve.

Seeing it now, resurrected after years of suppression under communism, is to witness a dedication to renewal and the Ukrainian peoples' deeply held religious conviction that lay dormant but never really went away.

The complex has two sections, the Upper Lavra with its museums and buildings considered of national importance, and the Lower Lavra, a working monastery and site of the caves that give it its name.

Excavated from the soft sandstone and loess, the caves are a labyrinthine web of tunnels, passages, monastic cells, chapels, churches and catacombs where mummified bodies of monks and saints, preserved by the cool humid atmosphere and viewed in glass-topped coffins, tuck into niches along the walls.

The caves get very crowded and they are not the place for claustrophobics. But to follow the headscarved faithful winding their way through the narrow passages, lit only by hand-held candles and a few sanctuary lamps, is to experience an atmosphere of intense spirituality. This is especially true of the Far Caves, which receive far fewer foreign tourists.

In 1051, Anthony, an Eastern Orthodox monk, returned from Mount Athos in Greece and settled in a hillside cave on the bank of the Dnieper River, where a community soon grew up around him and the Far Caves, as they are now known, expanded rapidly.

Having established a monastery and appointed a hegumen (abbot), Anthony withdrew from the community

Photo: Jorge Láscar

and dug out a new underground cell on a hill. This area, too, grew to accommodate many monks. Now known as the Near Caves, here there are churches and chapels below and above ground, including the underground Church of Saint Anthony. There is also a bell tower at the bottom of the hill.

The most important church in the Near Caves area is the Baroque-style Church of the Elevation of the Cross, erected at the turn of the 18th century. Its carved and gilded three-tier iconostasis is spectacular.

Nearby, the long, green-roofed Refectory Church, built in Neo-Classical style in 1895 when more than 1,000 monks were living in the lavra, has a huge Byzantine-style dome layered in gold and surrounded by bulbous gold-topped towers above a columned portico.

The main entrance to the monastery is impressive. Murals of saintly monks lead towards the flamboyantly colourful, decidedly Baroque, Gate Church of the Trinity that towers atop the Holy Gates. Panels of gold-haloed saints fill the façade, the gilded cupola glitters in the sunlight and inside are frescoes based on biblical scenes and Ukrainian folklore.

Once inside the lavra's 28 hectare estate the view is of golden domes and glittering crosses, gleaming white walls and frescoed niches, green roofs, Baroque bonnets and tree-lined streets busy with people. Museums display wondrous treasures, from Scythian gold and exquisite jewellery to rare ancient books and manuscripts.

The history of the Dormition (Assumption) Cathedral, the main church of the lavra, goes back to its foundation in 1073. Very little remained of what had been a magnificent Byzantine-influenced structure after it was mined and blown up by retreating Soviet troops during the Second World War. Reconstruction began in 1998 and the building was re-consecrated during the Ukrainian Independence

Day ceremonies of August 2000, although work on the decoration has lasted for years since. Huge and spectacular, its outer walls, white painted, iced with gold and inset with tiers of paintings, hint at the glorious frescoes and icons to be discovered within.

Like a wedding cake, with four tiers and a gilded dome, the blue and white Great Lavra Bell Tower reaches heavenwards in Classical style, supported by decorated columns. In the centre of Cathedral Square, it has a viewing platform on the third tier and above that the chiming clock, its design based on the Moscow Kremlin clock, has stopped only once in its existence – in 1944 when the lavra's Dormition Cathedral was blown up.

It's easy to spend a day here exploring the churches and caves, making discoveries in museums and enjoying the gardens. It's a world away from the forest of concrete tower blocks seen on the far bank of the river. Kiev's Monastery of the Caves is an intensely atmospheric place to visit.

– AUSTRALIA –

ST MARY'S CATHEDRAL, SYDNEY

The story of the Cathedral Church and Minor Basilica of the Immaculate Mother of God, Help of Christians is inextricably linked with the history of Australia.

Established as a penal settlement in 1788, the chaplain of the colony was a Church of England minister. Many of the convicts and settlers were Roman Catholics, but it wasn't until 1820 that the first official Catholic chaplains arrived –

Father John Therry, who stayed in Sydney, and Father Philip Connelly who went on to Van Diemen's Land (Tasmania).

Father Therry petitioned the Governor, Lacklan Macquarie, for land on which to build a chapel and he wasn't best pleased with what he was offered. It was on the edge of town, close to the convict barracks on the edge of Hyde Park, an empty field where the sandstone bricks for Macquarie's new buildings were being made.

Not a great location back then, but today the area is at the heart of the city, surrounded by the high-rises of Sydney's central business district and Hyde Park's avenues of trees, fountains and formal gardens, with the elegant Neo-Gothic St Mary's Cathedral a much-loved city landmark.

From the moment he stepped ashore, Father Therry had a vision of a chapel 'with spires pointing to heaven as a pledge of hope to a flock that is almost without hope, the Catholic convicts'. It would come about, but the spires would take 180 years to materialise.

Governor Macquarie laid the foundation stone in 1821 and a church complex developed, with the first Mass celebrated in the church in 1833. It was elevated to the status of cathedral on the arrival of Australia's first Catholic bishop in 1835 (in 1930, Pope Pius XI gave it the title of a Minor Basilica). The church was large and Neo-Gothic in design with input from the English Gothic Revivalist architect, Augustus Pugin. Father Therry died in 1864 and a year later, on 29 June 1865, disaster stuck as fire swept through the buildings and destroyed the cathedral.

In the autumn of that year, the architect William Wilkinson Wardell was approached to build an even bigger and more impressive cathedral on the site.

A keen Gothic Revivalist and friend of Pugin, Wardell had immigrated to Australia from England seven years earlier and was making a name for himself in Melbourne. His design was indeed of very impressive proportions and because of its size and the contours of the land, the cathedral had to be built facing north–south rather than the traditional liturgical east–west orientation.

The foundation stone was laid in December 1868 and the rest built in sections until 1928. Officially opened in 1900, the cathedral was consecrated to Our Lady, Help of Christians (the patroness of Australia) in 1905, when Sydney's Archbishop, Cardinal Patrick Moran, described it as 'a gift from the poor' because they had donated most of the money raised to build it. Archbishops and bishops representing every diocese in Australia attended the ceremony.

Constructed from local golden-brown sandstone, St Mary's is the largest Gothic cathedral in the southern hemisphere, even dwarfing some of the European models that inspired it, and the longest ecclesiastical building in Australia.

With flying buttresses and a sturdy bell tower defined by delicate crocketed pinnacles, it presents a pleasing profile, full of decorative Gothic details. The 75-metre (246-foot)-tall spires Wardell had intended (and Father Therry had envisioned), a scheme that had been abandoned for lack of funds, were finally constructed and put in place for the millennium in 2000.

Neo-Gothic in the style of late 13th-century England, in particular Lincoln Cathedral (page 24), St Mary's has a conventional English cathedral plan, cruciform with a tower over the crossing of the nave and transepts and twin towers at the west front (except that here, due to the orientation of the site, it is the south front). Light comes from stained glass windows in the aisles and from the three overhead rose windows. The tracery of the huge chancel window is almost a copy of that at Lincoln.

Photo: Diego Delso

Unlike the interior, which is based on mainly English architectural features, the main entrance façade with its three huge portals and central rose window is reminiscent of the Gothic west front of Notre-Dame Cathedral in Paris.

Stone carvings depicting Australian native plants, including the waratah, the floral emblem of New South Wales, surround the doors of the Hyde Park entrance. Here you'll find a statue of Australia's first and only saint, Mary MacKillop. Canonised in 2010, she was given the name St Mary of the Cross.

The high central nave, flanked by an aisle on either side, rises to three storeys of towering pillars and graceful pointed arches beneath a vaulted roof of red cedar wood. The chancel's timber vaulting may originally have been planned to be richly decorated like that of Peterborough Cathedral (page 53) but it remains unpainted.

Behind the high altar, the delicately carved screen in Oamaru limestone from New Zealand has statue-filled niches. Side chapels, too, have ornately carved reredos behind their altars. The relief sculpture on the low altar's marble frontal has been controversial. Inspired by the Shroud of Turin and depicting Christ dead in the tomb, it was dedicated by Pope Benedict XVI on his visit to Sydney in 2008.

The stained glass windows are superb. Spanning a period of some 50 years and ranging in style from the 19th-century Gothic Revival to the more painterly feeling of the early 20th century, they culminate in the huge and magnificent chancel window. Depicting the Downfall of Humanity, the central figures are Christ seated in judgement with Mary, crowned and enthroned beside him, pleading for mercy on Christians.

The powerfully realistic sculpture on the Grave of the Unknown Soldier was the work of George Washington

Lambert, a portraitist and First World War artist who had immigrated with his mother and sisters to Australia in 1887. Over in the western transept, the marble replica of Michelangelo's Pietá sculpture has an unusual provenance. It was brought to Australia for display in a Sydney department store and later donated to the cathedral.

Below, the vaulted crypt has the tombs of pioneer priests and five archbishops of Sydney as well as an interesting exhibition on the beginnings and growth of the Catholic community in Sydney. In the memorial chapels, marble altars have bas-reliefs and carvings, a ceiling is painted with Australian native flora and stained glass windows depict defining events in the life of the Virgin Mary.

But the main reason for going down there is to see the floor, which is sensational.

Crafted in terrazzo and marble, and only completed in 1961, it was inspired by the *Book of Kells*, the 9th-century illuminated manuscript of the four Gospels that is Ireland's greatest cultural treasure.

Full of exuberant colour, the floor design features a huge Celtic cross in a heady mix of complex swirls, geometric shapes and twisted rope designs. Five large medallions placed around the cross depict the creation of the world as described in the Book of Genesis, while eighteen smaller medallions represent the titles of the Immaculate Mother of God, to whom the cathedral is dedicated.

AFRICA

– ETHIOPIA –

THE ROCK-HEWN CHURCHES OF LALIBELA

Lalibela is one of the world's most remarkable places and its eleven churches, excavated out of solid red volcanic rock, are among the most unusual and extraordinary structures to be found anywhere. Hidden away in the mountains of northern Ethiopia, this is one of the holiest places in the Ethiopian Orthodox Church.

Always a place of pilgrimage, Lalibela's churches are in constant use. Every day, in the chill mist of dawn, people wrapped in their white, homespun cotton muslin clothes climb hills and trek across stony, mud-worn mountain paths to pray. It is a scene unchanged for centuries. Even the rituals seem frozen in time, for they are conducted in Ge'ez, an ancient language few people would understand today. Accompanied by the beating of drums and chanting, worship can last for hours.

Dating from the late 12th or early 13th centuries, each church is carved in one piece out of the red volcanic rock in which it stands. Most have their roof at ground level.

Reached by rough-cut, often steep stairs descending into narrow trenches they lie, almost hidden, glowing pink-red in the earth. Set in courtyards and linked by tunnels and labyrinthine passages, their interiors are chiselled into decorated windows, pilasters, columns and arches, their floors worn uneven by the bare feet of worshippers over centuries. Hermits' caves and catacombs, too, have been dug out from rock walls.

At almost 40 metres (130 feet) long, 24 metres (78 feet) wide and 12 metres (40 feet) high, Bet Medhane Alem, House of the Redeemer of the World, is the largest of the churches. It has a colonnade around it, reminiscent of a Greek temple. Inside, sunbeams cast shadowy light on a sea of square columns and capitals under a barrel-vaulted nave and four aisles and reveal the simplicity and harmony of a basilica.

Each church is different. One has porches, a vaulted nave and two aisles, galleries like low passageways and a domed sanctuary; several are decorated with wall paintings.

They are clustered in two main groups, one on each side of a torrent bed known as the River Jordan and separated by village houses. The amazingly sophisticated Bet Giyorgis (St George's Church) stands alone, dug from a sloping plateau of rock. Built in the shape of a cross and perfectly proportioned, it rises tower-like from its stepped plinth 12 metres (40 feet) down.

Standing at the edge of its deep pit you look upon a roof design of three equilateral Greek crosses inside each other. Uneven steps and a long, baked mud passage bring you down to its entrance. Graves of pious monks and pilgrims lie in caves and chambers in the courtyard walls. Inside, Bet Giyorgis is comparatively plain but has intricately carved reliefs, decorated columns and Christian images, including the saint to whom the church is dedicated. A curtain shields the Holy of Holies; the shadowy transept displays the church's Tabot (replica of the Ark of the Covenant).

Of the three churches set around a large courtyard, Bet Mariam (St Mary's Church) is the smallest but has the most interesting design and decoration. Above the western porch, a rare and finely carved bas-relief of St George

fighting the dragon tucks in beneath the roof. Inside, the ceilings and upper walls are painted with early frescoes and the columns, capitals and arches are beautifully carved. Representing the Holy Trinity and the Crucifixion, two vertical sets of three windows punctuate the east wall and illuminate the Holy of Holies.

Nearby are the twin churches of Bet Mikael, known for its cruciform pillars and plethora of relief-carved crosses, and Bet Golgotha. Sadly for women, who would be equally keen to see its Early Christian art and life-sized depictions of the twelve Apostles, only men are allowed in to Bet Golgotha, which contains the curtained Selassie Chapel, a holy sanctuary said to contain the tomb of the saintly King.

King Lalibela gave the town its name (it was previously known as Roha) and its churches. Born into the Zagwe dynasty, when a swarm of bees attended his birth his mother believed it was a sign that one day her son would rule Ethiopia. The name she gave him means 'the bees recognise his sovereignty'.

Legend says that God instructed King Lalibela to build churches unlike any others and in his vision of a New Jerusalem in the Ethiopian mountains, the king built his churches not as would be expected, in bricks and stone from the ground up, but from deep into the ground itself. While archaeologists believe it took thousands of men several decades to create the eleven churches, the popular legend insists it took 23 years with the king working by day and the angels taking over at night.

The dusty, rural town is a busy place and the huge Saturday market is packed with the produce of local farmers who till stony ground with the traditional hook plough. In this austere, steeply mountainous terrain, every possible inch of land is cultivated. Isolated, always difficult to reach, before the tarmac road from the airport was built the town was completely cut off during the rainy season.

This nation embraced Christianity in the 4th century, making it the state religion in 330 AD. To see the depth of the people's spirituality today at Lalibela is very moving.

At Ganna (Christmas) on 7 January the joyful, all-night celebrations, especially at Bet Mariam, are emotionally involving. Timkat (Ephipany) on 19 January is the most important festival, when tens of thousands of white-robed pilgrims descend on Lalibela for three days of colourful ceremonies unique in the world. Many will have walked for days and weeks to be there.

NORTH AMERICA

– CANADA –

NOTRE-DAME BASILICA, MONTRÉAL

Entering the Basilique Notre-Dame-de-Montréal for the first time is a catch-your-breath moment. Under a soaring midnight-blue ceiling spattered with gold stars brighter than the night sky, it is a dazzling vision of colour in the carved wood, sculptures, painted and patterned columns and stained glass windows.

In the heart of the city's oldest neighbourhood and named after its first parish, Notre-Dame, the Mother Church of

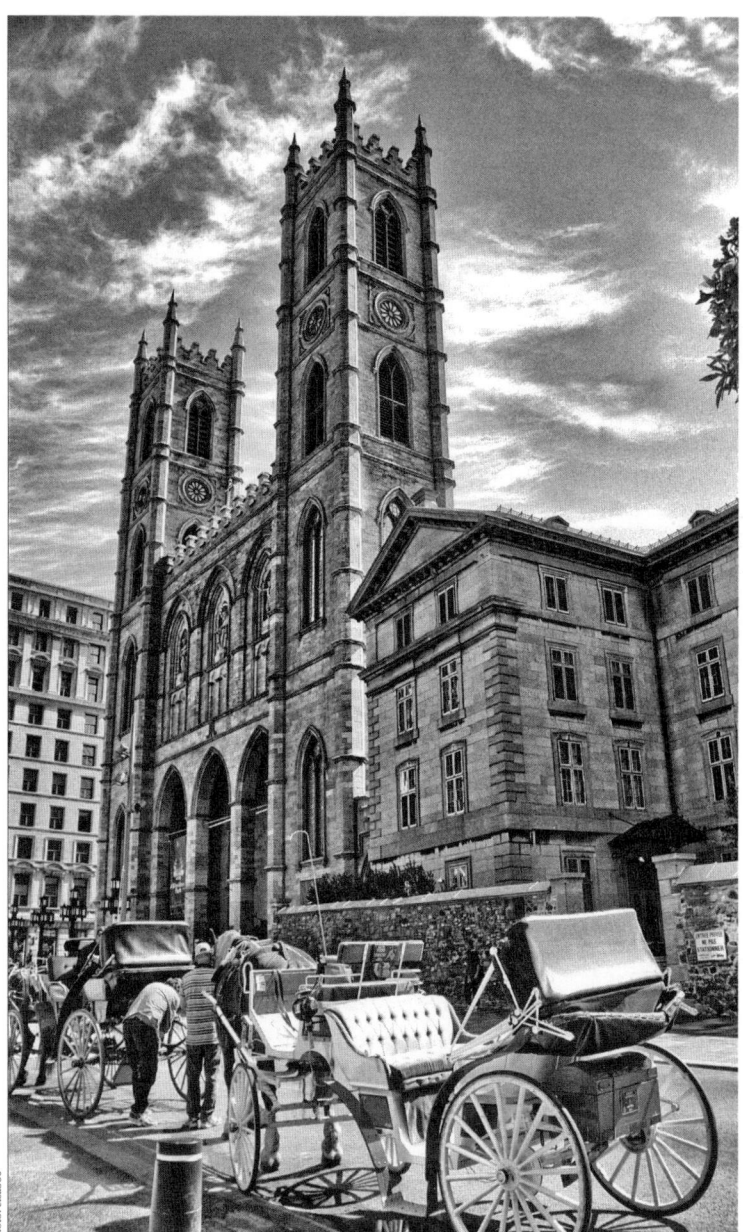

Montréal was built in 1824 to replace the smaller 17th-century parish church where the first settlers had worshipped.

With decorative pointed arches, parapet and pinnacles, 70-metre (228-foot)-tall twin squared towers (nicknamed Temperance and Perseverance) and the interior inspired by the Sainte-Chapelle in Paris, the immense stone church was the largest house of worship in North America at the time.

Designed by James O'Donnell, an Irish-American Protestant architect from New York, it was also the first significant example of the Gothic Revival style in Canada, a style that would go on to gain prominence in church architecture across the country. Pope John Paul II raised the status of the church to that of minor basilica in 1982 and visited in 1984.

Everything about this basilica is big and bold. It can accommodate up to 10,000 people, the eleven-tonne bass bell (cast in England and raised into position using cables and pulley blocks borrowed from a railway company) is the largest in North America and the great Casavant organ with 92 stops and 7,000 pipes can make a sound like no other.

The simple, rectangular floor plan of nave and galleries is dominated by the dramatic high altar, intricately carved, gilded and painted, its niches filled with statues.

The Crucifixion stands at the centre of the altarpiece; around it are Old Testament scenes that prefigure the sacrifice of the Cross and the Mass. Beneath the altar, a wood carving of the Last Supper is based on the Leonardo da Vinci mural in Milan. Angels and saints, bas-relief sculptures in wood, surround the tabernacle and above them all, is the Coronation of the Blessed Virgin.

Curving over the choir stalls, painted statues of Saints Peter and Paul and the evangelists Matthew, Mark, Luke and John are framed in Gothic arches. Skilfully carved pinnacles and spires rise heavenwards against a backdrop of the blue colour that makes the church and its altar so distinctive.

Given a magnificent curving staircase, the pulpit, too, is stunningly ornate, towering above the congregation in a feast of carving, with seated figures of the Old Testament prophets Ezekiel and Jeremiah at its feet. A dove, symbol of the Holy Spirit, appears in the brightly lit overhead canopy graced by the figures of four Fathers of the Church.

Canada's first native-born saint, Marguerite d'Youville and the county's first schoolteacher, St Marguerite Bourgeoys have side altars dedicated to them. Behind the main altar, the smaller but equally colourful Chapelle du Sacré Coeur (Chapel of the Sacred Heart) is a popular venue for weddings. Its massive altarpiece of 32 sculpted bronze panels was the work of the noted Québec artist Charles Daudelin.

Some of the region's finest artists, sculptors and craftspeople contributed to the decoration of the basilica. The stained glass windows along the walls of the sanctuary were installed to mark Notre-Dame's centenary in 1929. Designed by a local artist and made in Limoges, France, they depict scenes from the early days of Montréal's settlement (Ville-Marie as it was first called) and its social and religious history.

The fine acoustics make Notre Dame an ideal location for summer season concerts by renowned orchestras and its organ is the focus of the annual International Organ Festival.

From the great columns and their capitals to the ribbed vaults and carved fronts of the galleries, no surface seems untouched by the vibrant (some might say brash) colours. This huge church has impact and once seen is difficult to forget.

– USA –

WASHINGTON NATIONAL CATHEDRAL, WASHINGTON DC

At the highest point of the nation's capital, the Cathedral Church of St Peter and St Paul in Washington, DC, is a 20th-century 'spiritual home for the nation' and 'house of prayer for all people'.

It has seen the state funerals of three US presidents and Presidential prayer services held after the six inaugurations between 1937 (President Roosevelt) and 2017 (President Trump) as well as many national memorial services and celebrations. Its dramatic Gothic outline stands out on the skyline of a city better known for its Neo-Classical architecture.

In 1907, President Theodore Roosevelt laid the foundation stone on which the crypt's Bethlehem Chapel of the Nativity was built. Five years later the cathedral's first service was held there and ever since it has been the setting for the first of the three services held each day (four on Sunday).

The final piece of stone, a finial, was hauled into place in the presence of President George H.W. Bush in 1990, though decorative work continued well after that 'official' completion. In August 2011 an earthquake caused $26 million damage to the cathedral's stonework that is likely to take a decade to repair.

Eighty-three years does not seem an excessive length of time to create a building of such size and grandeur. It was constructed in the manner of the medieval cathedrals, stone on stone, without such modern support assistance as structural steel.

Built of Indiana limestone, cruciform in shape with a long nave, wide side aisles and transepts, its pointed arches, bosses, ribbed vaulting, large windows and flying buttresses are all designed to lift the eye upwards. Above the crossing, adorned with 388 carved angel heads, the Gloria in Excelsis Tower has two full sets of bells – a 53-bell carillon and a ten-bell peal for ringing changes – which is unique in North America.

The nine-bay nave has a calming elegance in its cool cream stone, smoothly carved columns and graceful arches. It can seat over 3,200 people and is so long that the Washington Monument could be laid down in its attractively patterned marble aisle.

The interior is a showcase of fine craftsmanship that celebrates biblical events and pays tribute to America's finest hours, history and heroes. All the decorative details have a story to tell and the 231 stained glass windows are superb.

Famed for their depth of colour, clarity and sparkle, they range from the powerful Sacrifice for Freedom windows in the War Memorial Chapel to the delightful window extolling the virtues of Martha Washington. A tiny piece of the moon, plucked from the Sea of Tranquillity and delivered personally by the Apollo 11 astronauts who brought it back, is set in a capsule amid the whirling stars and orbiting planets in the Space Window.

The abstract Creation rose, 8 metres (25 feet) in diameter and one of three glorious rose windows, bathes the nave with colour. A life-sized figure of Christ sits in Judgement in the north transept's rose window and in the south transept, the Church Triumphant window has imagery from the Book of Revelation. In contrast to their vibrancy, the Bethlehem Chapel's fine stained glass has a darker, medieval feel.

Symbolism is never far away. The stone for the splendid Canterbury Pulpit, intricately carved with people and

Photo: Carol M. Highsmith

scenes relating to the translation of the Bible into English, was originally part of the Bell Harry Tower at Canterbury Cathedral (page 18). The high altar, known as the Jerusalem Altar, is made from twelve stones from the Solomon Quarry near Jerusalem. In the floor in front of the altar are ten stones from the Chapel of Moses on Mount Sinai – symbolically, then, the altar stands founded on the Ten Commandments. The ruins of England's legendary Glastonbury Abbey provided the stone for the cathedra, the Bishop's seat.

Look around to see screens of finely carved wood and intricate wrought iron, murals, fabric art and colourful needlepoint kneelers in all the chapels. The mosaics in the Resurrection Chapel, depicting Christ's appearances from Easter morning to Ascension Day, gleam in multi-shades of glass against their gold background.

There's George Washington in Vermont marble, Abraham Lincoln in bronze, and the tomb of Thomas Woodrow Wilson, the only American president to be buried in Washington, DC.

Music plays an important role in the life of the cathedral and the impressive 10,650-pipe organ accompanies its noted choirs.

Thousands of fanciful stone carvings cover the exterior. Over 1,000 grotesques – including *Star Wars'* villain Darth Vader, though you'll need binoculars to spot him – are carved so rainwater will drop off their noses and 112 gargoyles (look for the hippy with ripped jeans) drain water through their spouting mouths.

The Bishop's walled garden, designed by the son of the landscape architect of New York's Central Park, is a place of quiet amid magnolia and yew trees, roses and herbs and has paths of stone from George Washington's quarries.

For a panoramic view from the top of the cathedral, just take the elevator to the Pilgrim Observation Gallery spanning the two west towers.

SOUTH AMERICA

– BRAZIL –

METROPOLITAN CATHEDRAL, RIO DE JANEIRO

Call it Modernist or Brutalist, love it or hate it, one thing's for sure, the Catedral Metropolitana de São Sebastião is different.

Its conical shape is said to have been inspired by ancient Mayan pyramids in Mexico (although its base is circular, not square as in the Mayan temples). From the outside the four enormous, curved and latticed sides appear as a concrete honeycomb of square windows and give no inkling of the colour inside.

Designed by architect Edgar Fonseca, dedicated to the city's patron saint and built between 1964 and 1976 during the time of the military dictatorship, politics aside it was always going to be controversial.

Life-sized statues flank the stairs to the main entrance, where 48 bronze reliefs cover the doors. Cool, polished concrete leads into the spectacular interior. In the centre of each wall, vividly coloured window panels rise into the arms of a translucent Greek cross that's set into a flat circular roof 30 metres (98 feet) in diameter. The cross symbolises the presence of Christ among men and the 65-metre

Photo: Ezarate

(213-foot)-tall panels represent 'the one, holy, Catholic and Apostolic Church'.

Facing south, the green window has symbols of unity and faith: the Bible, the bishop's mitre, the Papal tiara, the chalice and the Host. In the red window, looking east, images of the Virgin Mary and Saint Joseph join the sufferings of Christ, the redemption of sins and the descent of the Holy Spirit. Above the main entrance in the blue window, symbols of the Evangelists with their Gospels, a globe and a cross present the Catholic faith as universal, while the yellow window looks west and is all about the propagation of faith with St Peter holding the keys.

The contemplative aura of this mammoth cathedral, which can seat 5,000 worshippers (the standing room capacity is 20,000), is a welcome respite after the traffic-heavy Centro streets that surround it. Recordings of Gregorian chant echo within the soaring space. Pope Francis celebrated Mass here on World Youth Day in July 2013.

A giant wooden cross, held aloft by six steel cables, hangs above the raised high altar that's large enough to seat a full orchestra. São Paulo sculptor Humberto Cozzo's striking statue of St Francis holding a dove in his outstretched hand is a standout piece among the modern sculptures.

In the basement, the collection of sculptures, murals and artwork in the Museum of Sacred Art features the fountain used for the Portuguese royal family's baptisms and the Golden Rose given by Pope Leo XIII to Princess Isabel in celebration of the signing of the Lei Áurea, which abolished slavery in Brazil.

Rio's downtown Metropolitana, often referred to as the 'new' cathedral, stands in stark contrast to the 'old' cathedral. Several churches had been designated a cathedral in the past and with the arrival of the Portuguese Royal Court in

1808, in flight from Napoleon's invading troops, it was the Igreja Nossa Senhora do Monte do Carmo (Church of Our Lady of Mount Carmel) that took the title and doubled as the Imperial Chapel.

Theatrical in its colours and Rococo decor, the old Carmelite church saw royal and imperial weddings, baptisms, funerals, coronations and religious ceremonies of state. When the then Archbishop of Rio was elevated to the status of cardinal in 1905, it became the first seat of a cardinal in Brazil.

The city's first church, Igreja Nossa Senhora da Candelária, dates from 1630 but only the elegant façade hints of its history. Its 19th-century, marble-clad, Neo-Classical interior is a feast of vividly coloured stained glass, rich bronze and glorious painted ceilings. Some of these tell the story of Antônio de Palma and his wife who, in thanksgiving for having survived the storm that threatened to wreck their ship, built a chapel on this site in 1610.

The crowning dome, built from Portuguese limestone and decorated with eight white marble statues sculpted in Portugal, stands out amid the city high-rises that surround the church. Its bronze door panels, cast in France, were originally exhibited at the 1889 World's Fair in Paris.

Overlooking Glória marina and on the site of the founding of the city, the pretty little 18th-century Igreja da Nossa Senhora da Glória do Outeiro, known much more simply as Igreja da Glória (Gloria Church), is a favourite among Rio locals.

The sight of its single bell tower was said to revive hope for the sailors coming into the bay. Octagonal in shape, its beautiful interior of Rococo woodcarving and Portuguese blue *azulejos* (tiles) is considered one of the most important examples of colonial religious architecture in Brazil.

The unassuming colonial façade of the hilltop São Bento Monastery belies its exuberant Baroque interior. Glinting top-to-toe in gold, every surface is covered in ornate carvings and the giant silver chandeliers each weigh in at 136 kilograms (300 lb). Still a working Benedictine monastery, the monks' Sunday morning Masses are a must for lovers of church music.

NOTES

NOTES

NOTES

NOTES